What People Are Saying About

Lots To Do In Line Disneyland

"Part trivia, part eye spy, and entirely fun."
— Jason Dziegielewski, Disney Geek

"Pick up your copy … and start experiencing the lines at Disneyland rather than enduring them!"
— Natalie Henley, Meet The Magic

"The book has things to find…for every single ride. …Everyone around us in line wanted to join in the fun!"
— A Mom's Take

"Makes an interactive experience out of every queue in Disneyland…that will happily occupy any person waiting in line. … Definitely a must-have."
— James Dolan, The Disney Driven Life

"The perfect book to prevent meltdowns when you're with a group of people on a relatively busy day at Disneyland."
— Sam Gennawey, Samland Library Of Dreams

"When you are stuck in line with kids you NEED something to do. … Great book."
— Caren Kristine, As The Spine Breaks

"Captures the playful and fantastical essence of Disney. … A great…way to keep your entire family engaged in the Disney experience."
ids

"There's some   joy,
look at, answ   …
Check it out!"

— Chad & Mark, Days In The Park

Lots To Do In Line: Disneyland

Second Edition

Meredith Lyn Pierce

Lots To Do In Line: Disneyland
2nd Edition

Published by
The Intrepid Traveler
P.O. Box 531
Branford, CT 06405
http://intrepidtraveler.com

Cover design by George Foster, FosterCovers.com
Interior Design by Tim Foster, tgfDesign.com
Library of Congress Control Number: 2013940373
ISBN13: 978-1-937011-37-6

10 9 8 7 6 5 4 3 2 1

Trademarks, Etc.

Dedication

This book is dedicated to the great loves of my life: my husband Ken, my mother Carol, and last but not least, my daughter Camille. There are a million reasons for this dedication but let's settle for you make my life unbelievably wonderful.

It is also dedicated to my grandfather Philip Crawford, who told me I was meant to be a writer.

Table of Contents

Disney California Adventure Park, cont'd.

Enjoy the Fun Before the Ride

Welcome to the "happiest place on earth." You are in for a wonderful time. If you are a child, or a child at heart, the fun is everywhere. Many guidebooks have been written about Disneyland and I have no intention of writing "just another guidebook." I wrote "Lots To Do In Line Disneyland" to celebrate the fun that most people overlook on their visit to Disney's magical kingdom—the lines. That's right, the lines. Puzzled? Read on.

As you are doubtless aware, lines at the Disneyland parks tend to be daunting much of the year. No one likes to stand and wait. But happily, you don't have to just stand and wait at the Disneyland parks. Disney's Imagineers have packed a wealth of detail and delight in just about every queue line in the park. All you need to do is open your eyes and your imagination.

With this book as your guide, a writing implement in hand, and a child (or a child at heart) by your side ready to play, you'll be all set to make your time in line some of your happiest memories of your visit. Disney provides all the rest, with occasional help from your fellow guests.

How Do I Use This Book?

"Lots To Do In Line" turns your wait time into fun time by using the wealth of visual (and sometimes audio) detail Disney builds into its parks and most of its queue lines to create games for each ride in Disneyland and Disney California Adventure. The rides are grouped alphabetically in the "lands" and "areas" found in the official park Guidemaps (see the Index in the back of this book for specific page numbers).

As you join a new queue, open your book to the appropriate ride. You'll find challenging questions and treasure hunts that turn time in line into an amusing game. You don't need any prior knowledge to play these games. All the answers can be found just by looking around you, in the queue and beyond, for those clever details the Disney Imagineers and designers have provided. The questions are multiple-choice, meaning you never need to stop to fill in an answer, and the hunts ask you to circle or check the items you find, so again, you have nothing to write in.

Waiting times vary, of course, and some ride queues are less well detailed than others. To ensure that you have fun all the way up to the loading dock, you will sometimes be directed to build a "Collection." Collections are groups of things to look for that you'll find sprinkled all around the parks (weather vanes, for example) or things you can spot on your fellow guests, such as sparkling shoes and character T-shirts. You can hunt for Collection treasure anytime you choose, while in line or while walking around the parks. "Collection Suggestions," page 13, offers a list of things you might "collect" in your day in the park, but feel free to use your imagination.

Earn Points

Let's face it, everything is more fun when you get points for it. You get 1 point for every question you answer correctly. You also get 1 point for every item you find when treasure hunting and 1 point every time you add an item to one of your Collections. In addition, at the end of the day, you get 5 bonus points for every Collection in which you've gathered more than 10 items. If you pay close attention, Collections will help you clean up on points. Remember, the more you get involved in having fun at Disneyland, the more points you'll rack up.

What do you get for your points? You get the joy of achieving them, of course! It's a great feeling to know you're succeeding—and you'll have the extra joy of seeing all the wonderful details that make the Disney parks so entertaining.

Three Ways To Play The Lots-To-Do Games

1) Team up with other members of your group to answer as many questions as possible. You've undoubtedly heard the saying "two minds are better than one." Well that is certainly true here. If everyone works together, your team can earn the most points and become experts in line-ology. You can add up your points for each queue line—and declare a winning team for each queue. Or you can add up all your points for the park at the end of the day to see how each team did overall. Or both.

2) Compete individually with other members of your group. Whoever answers the most questions correctly before you reach the end of the queue gets the most points and is declared the winner. (This method works best when each player has a copy of the book.)

3) Play the games without competing. You or your child may simply want to use this guide to enjoy all the special details in the queue lines. Of course, players must be able to read on their own to investigate the queues independently. Younger players will require the assistance of an adult or older friend or sibling.

Pop Quizzes

When you come to any place in the book marked **? POP QUIZ!**, you are about to play a memory game. I can sense you sweating it right now. Don't worry, there is no grade. This test is just for fun! The instructions will direct you to have a quick look at something before you get in line. Whatever it is will be very close at hand. After you look, join the queue and prepare to have some fun remembering what you saw.

Tip: Many of the pop quizzes involve the sign for the attraction, so always have a good look at it as you head for the queue.

Order Of The Questions

Where possible, questions are presented in the order you're likely to encounter the visuals or audio to answer them. In this way, the clues are sprinkled throughout the queue lines. Keep checking the next few questions ahead in case you pass something without noticing it. If you think you've passed by a clue, don't worry, it means you're getting closer to the ride.

By the way, while every effort has been made to present the questions in the order you will discover the clues, it is important to remember that queue lines are sometimes rearranged to accommodate larger crowds. In the event that the questions don't seem to match what you are seeing or hearing as you move through the queue, you can assume that the line has been rearranged—especially if you are visiting at a busy season, such as a holiday. Read ahead to find the questions applicable to the area you are currently in.

Using Lots To Do In FASTPASS Lines

Most of the time when you're waiting for rides, you will be standing in what Disney calls the Standby queues. These are the "regular" lines, the queues you simply walk into and move along until you reach the loading area for the ride. A few of the most popular rides offer FASTPASS options. These are special queues with shorter waits. (The Guidemap you are given when you enter the park tells you exactly how they work.)

When you are using a FASTPASS, you won't see everything that you would see from the Standby line because you will bypass much of the queue. So when you use FASTPASS, look for the questions marked **FP**. The clues for these questions are visible from both the Standby and FASTPASS queues unless otherwise noted. In most cases though, the FASTPASS line will move so quickly that you will only be able to answer a few questions at most.

Scan the questions marked **FP** to find ones that correspond to your location in the FASTPASS line.

A Special Note For Grown-ups

Most people, regardless of age, truly hate waiting in line and children find it particularly daunting because the very nature of a child is to be active. They are learning, thinking, seeing, and doing beings. They are never sedentary. Children do not just "look and enjoy," they "do" things. So while everything you need to stay happy and entertained is right there for you in most of the queues, it's easy for children (and many older folk, as well) to miss them. That's where this book comes in.

"Lots To Do In Line" will help you and your child experience the Disneyland theme park queues actively, turning the wait into a game. Instead of asking kids to appreciate, say, an interesting prop when they come to it, it will have them hunting for that prop, trying to discover something about it, and earning points for their accomplishments. And let's face it, adults and teens enjoy that, too; this book is designed to keep the whole family interested.

The questions are intended to offer a challenge but not to be so hard that a child feels he or she is losing the game. To that end, the multiple-choice design provides hints as to where to look to find the answer successfully. Disneyland, after all, is designed to be "the happiest place on earth," not a place to lose. While children are focused on a quest, they can't be complaining of being bored, hot, or hungry.

Happy kids at Disneyland equal happy parents. Have a great time enjoying the challenges.

— Meredith Pierce

P.S. The Disneyland parks are constantly changing—adding new attractions and renovating and replacing others. So it is likely that when you visit, a few of the queue clues will have changed. If you spot things that are no longer there—or new things that have been added, I hope your will let me know care of my website, LotsToDoInLine.com. Sharing what you know will make these games even more fun for everyone.

COLLECTION SUGGESTIONS

You should choose Collections that you think will work well for the area you are in. For example, if you are in Fantasyland, a Collection of girls dressed like princesses should serve you well. If you are in New Orleans Square, you will probably find a Collection of pirate flags more useful.

Some things, such as Mickey Mouse ears, are useful absolutely everywhere.

When you come to a ride that calls for Collections, choose several. Remember, you get 1 point for every item you add to a Collection and 5 bonus points at the end of the day for every Collection that includes more than 10 items.

1) Weather vanes. Many Disney rides have interesting weather vanes on top. If you look carefully you should find lots.

2) Hats. There are many funny hats for sale at Disneyland, and guests come with hats of their own. Earn 1 point for each different kind of hat you collect. For baseball caps, earn 1 point for each separate color you find.

3) Pin collectors. Many people visiting the parks will have collections of Disney Pins. These are fun to look at and easy to collect. Earn 1 point for each pin collector you spot.

4) Girls dressed as princesses. Young visitors sometimes like to get in the spirit by dressing as their favorite princess.

5) Crazy backpacks. There are all sorts of funny backpacks available at Disneyland. You can count ones you see in stores (only one of a kind, please) and ones people are wearing. See if you can spot anyone with a crazy backpack.

6) Pirate flags. It would appear that pirates have made their presence known at the Disneyland

Resort. If you keep your eyes open, you can find some of the places they have been, marked with their flag.

7) Different Mickey Mouse ears. Mickey ears come in many varieties. How many can you spot today?

8) Sparkling shoes. Time to check out the feet of your fellow guests. Some of them are glittery.

9) Shoes with no laces. As long as you are looking down already, see how many shoes without laces you can spot.

10) People wearing different Disney characters on their T-shirts. Many people like to wear Disney-character T-shirts while visiting the parks. How many different people wearing character T-shirts can you find?

11) Modes of transportation. Disneyland operates many kinds of vehicles. How many different kinds can you find?

12) Images of Disney characters. There are pictures and sculptures of characters from various movies all around the parks. How many can you collect?

13) People with balloons. You'll see lots of balloons at the Disneyland parks. How many people carrying a balloon can you spot? (If a person is carrying multiple balloons that only counts as one.)

14) Disney characters in the park. At various times, you'll see Disney characters in the theme parks greeting guests.

15) Cast iron stoves. There are a number of these in Disneyland Park's Frontierland and Adventureland.

16) Live ducks. You'll see many of these park residents enjoying the atmosphere and the bits of leftover food on the ground;

2 bonus points if you spot a live Donald Duck character.

17) Waterfalls. Keep your eyes and ears out for these. You get 2 points for each one.

18) Clock faces. There are many beautiful clocks around the parks. See how many you can find.

19) Water fountains. People get thirsty. Keep your eyes open for the water fountains.

20) Horsehead busts. There are a number of these to be found around Disneyland Park in the Main Street, U.S.A. area.

21) People with face paint. Yes. You can count yourself if you have your face painted—but only once.

22) People texting.

23) Kids dressed as pirates.

24) People with lightsabers.

Disneyland Park

Most of the challenges in this park take place strictly in the lines. However, there are times when you will be wandering around the park from one place to another. Perhaps you need a break or want to find a good lunch spot. For those times, turn to the Disneyland Park Scavenger Hunt at the end of this chapter.

Tip: You may want to read over the list now and then stay on the look-out. The treasures on the scavenger hunt list are scattered throughout the park. You get 1 point for every one you find.

Note: Unless specified otherwise, give yourself 1 point for each correct answer, 1 point for each Treasure you find, 1 point for each item you add to a Collection, and 1 point for any similar finds you make when you are hunting for something rather than answering a question. Good luck!

Main Street, U.S.A.

Disneyland Railroad Station

1. How much does it cost to get your weight?
   a. 25 cents
   b. 5 cents
   c. 1 penny
   d. 10 cents

2. Who was on the cover of *The Saturday Evening Post* on November 17, 1956?
   a. Snow White
   b. Pluto
   c. Walt Disney
   d. Pinocchio
   e. All of the above

3. What is the address of the fire department?
   a. 484
   b. 10
   c. 105
   d. 31

4. Find a detailed map of the route the Disneyland Railroad tracks follow. What is the name of the No. 2 train?
   a. Ernest S. Marsh
   b. E.P. Ripley
   c. Lilly Belle
   d. C.K. Holliday

5. What is the name of the full-sized train that was created using the Lilly Belle as a model?
   a. C.K. Holliday
   b. E.P. Ripley
   c. Ernest S. Marsh
   d. Fred Gurley

6. Treasure Hunt Time! It is time for a quick treasure hunt. Give yourself 1 point for each item you find from the list on page 20.

- ❏ A photograph of Walt Disney riding the miniature Lilly Belle in his backyard
- ❏ An antique child's admission ticket to Disneyland
- ❏ Four trunks
- ❏ The Golden Gate Bridge
- ❏ Grizzly Peak
- ❏ Tower of Terror
- ❏ The name of Walt Disney's daughter
- ❏ A map of California
- ❏ Bobbin Timer (You will know what it is when you find it.)
- ❏ A small model of the Lilly Belle

7. Collection Time! If you are still waiting to board your train, this is a great time to work on a Collection or two. Choose from Collections listed on page 13. Here are some that should work well on Main Street:

- ♦ Shoes with no laces
- ♦ People texting
- ♦ Mickey Mouse ears

Main Street, U.S.A. Answers

1) d. 10 cents
2) a. Snow White
3) c. 105
4) b. E.P. Ripley
5) a. C.K. Holliday
6) Total Treasures found _____
7) Number of items collected _____

Fantasyland

Alice in Wonderland

1. Which Alice in Wonderland characters are found on the giant book?
   - a. Alice
   - b. The White Rabbit
   - c. A talking flower
   - d. All of the above
   - e. Both 'a' and 'b'

2. The Mad Hatter's hat has a number on it. What is the number?
   - a. 8
   - b. 10/6
   - c. -6
   - d. 0.23

3. Who is having a birthday celebrated here today?
   - a. The Queen
   - b. Alice
   - c. Nobody
   - d. The White Rabbit, and he is late for it

4. What are the caterpillars traveling on?
   - a. Flowers
   - b. Leaves
   - c. Mushrooms
   - d. Grass

5. Who has lost part of his clothing?
   - a. The Caterpillar
   - b. The White Rabbit
   - c. The Mad Hatter
   - d. The Cheshire Cat

6. What garden plants are used for lights?
   - a. Mushrooms
   - b. Flowers
   - c. Leaves
   - d. All of the above

7. Treasure Hunt Time! Before you follow any rabbits down their holes, see if you can locate the following items. Better be fast; you wouldn't want to be late.

- ❑ A pocket watch
- ❑ A small horn
- ❑ A blue bow tie
- ❑ Confusing party-direction signs
- ❑ A napping caterpillar
- ❑ A heart wearing a crown
- ❑ Six yellow shoes
- ❑ A greeting to you
- ❑ Four pointing hands
- ❑ A garden creature who appears to be in a bad mood
- ❑ Alice's voice
- ❑ A small yellow mushroom with periwinkle spots

Casey Jr. Circus Train

1. Treasure Hunt Time! "Casey Jr." will be pulling into the station soon. See how many of the following items you can find before it is time for you to climb aboard.

- ❑ A dragon
- ❑ Golden rooftops that look like onions
- ❑ A home for monkeys
- ❑ A flotation ring
- ❑ A golden wing
- ❑ A tiny palm tree
- ❑ Flowery words
- ❑ Blue wheels
- ❑ A moving boat

2. Extra points!!! For 5 bonus points, how many times does the "Casey Jr." train come into view after it leaves the station?
   a. Three times and then it arrives at the station
   b. Twice and then it arrives at the station
   c. Four times and then it arrives at the station

3. Collection Time! If you are still waiting to board your train, this is a great time to work on a Collection or two. Here are some that should work well in Fantasyland:
   - People with face painting
   - People with balloons
   - Images of Disney characters

Or choose from the suggestions on page 13.

Dumbo the Flying Elephant

1. Treasure Hunt Time! Soon it will be time for you to ride on the back of your very own flying elephant. Before you do, see how many of the following items you can spot.
   - ❑ Pinwheels in pink and blue
   - ❑ An anchor
   - ❑ Four elephants balanced on a small ball
   - ❑ The letter D in a place of honor
   - ❑ A baby elephant
   - ❑ A whip
   - ❑ A teeny tiny rooftop skyline
   - ❑ Rodents doing cartwheels
   - ❑ A gold number 8
   - ❑ A topiary Dumbo
   - ❑ A big basket

2. Extra Points!!! For a bonus of 3 points, what is being given to one of the riders in each elephant and then taken away again?

    a. A peanut   b. A feather
    c. A mouse   d. Nothing

3. Collection Time! If you are still waiting to board your flying pachyderm, this is a great time to work on a Collection. If you've already started one, add to it. Or start a new one. Try weather vanes, hats, or crazy backpacks.

"it's a small world"

Entering "small world"

1. On what date did "small world" make its first voyage?

    a. 9/19/67   b. 4/22/64
    c. 11/25/67   d. 4/11/72

2. Which of the following animals is not growing in the garden?

    a. Elephant   b. Moose
    c. Bird   d. Dog
    e. Ostrich   f. They are all there.

3. "it's a small world" is a giant clock. There is another way to track time displayed on the front of the building that is not a clock. Can you find it?

    Yes / No

4. Find the doors. What are the doorknobs shaped like?

    a. Smiley faces   b. Pinwheels
    c. Flowers   d. Curlicues

5. There are two famous towers on the front of "small world." What are they? Chose two:
   a. The Leaning Tower of Pisa (a tower leaning to the side)
   b. The Tower of London (a large stone square with towers on all four corners)
   c. The Empire State Building (a thin, tall tower with a long point on the top)
   d. The Eiffel Tower (a tower with arches on the bottom)

6. What other ride goes through "it's a small world"?
   a. Storybook Land Canal Boats
   b. Disneyland Monorail
   c. Disneyland Railroad
   d. Only "small world" boats go through it.

7. How many pinwheels can you find? You get 1 point for each pinwheel you spot. _____

8. Treasure Hunt Time! There is a lot of glittery treasure to be found while you wait to embark on your trip around our small world. See how many you can find.
   ❏ Six gold drums
   ❏ A vase holding a flower
   ❏ A stack of four gold balls with the smallest one on the bottom
   ❏ A happy face
   ❏ The hands of a clock
   ❏ A cement ball
   ❏ A triangle standing on its tip
   ❏ A dolphin
   ❏ A corkscrew-shaped bush
   ❏ A gold bell
   ❏ A roof shaped like an onion
   ❏ Six gold flags
   ❏ Five clock gears
   ❏ A bridge

? Clock Parade Pop Quiz!

When the clock announces a time change, it's time to play Memory. Watch the parade very carefully. When it is over, see how many of these questions you can answer:

9. Did you see someone climb a mountain?
   Yes / No

10. Did you see a couple dancing together?
    Yes / No

11. Did you see someone hang ten?
    Yes / No

12. Was someone carrying a baby?
    Yes / No

13. Did you see someone who was dancing?
    Yes / No

14. Did you see someone with wooden shoes?
    Yes / No

15. Was there a lion jumping through a ring?
    Yes / No

16. Did you see someone riding a magic carpet?
    Yes / No

17. Was there a bride?
    Yes / No

18. Was someone riding a horse?
    Yes / No

19. Did you see someone playing the bagpipes?
    Yes / No

20. Did you see a four-leaf clover?
    Yes / No

21. Was someone playing the maracas?
    Yes / No

22. Was someone wearing fruit on her head?
    Yes / No

23. Was someone holding flowers?
    Yes / No

24. Was someone playing a violin?
    Yes / No

25. Was someone wearing a cowboy hat?
    Yes / No

26. Was there water?
    Yes / No

27. Was someone standing on his or her head?
    Yes / No

28. Did someone have on a grass skirt?
    Yes / No

29. Did someone have a boomerang?
    Yes / No

30. Was someone carrying a flag of his or her country?
    Yes / No

31. Did some of the people twirl while they moved?
    Yes / No

32. Was someone clapping?
    Yes / No

33. Did someone catch a fish?
    Yes / No

34. Did someone have a lasso?
    Yes / No

King Arthur Carrousel

1. What story is featured on the Carrousel?
   a. Cinderella   b. Snow White
   c. Sleeping Beauty   d. The Little Mermaid

2. What is on the top of the Carrousel's sign?
   a. A sword   b. A jewel
   c. A horse   d. A crown

3. Can you find animals to ride that are not horses?
   Yes / No

4. Do all of the horses have jewels on them?
   Yes / No

5. Is there a horse with a unicorn on its blanket?
   Yes / No

6. Is there a horse covered in bells?
   Yes / No

7. Is there a horse with a cherub on it?
   Yes / No

8. Is there one horse of a different color?
   Yes / No

9. Is there a horse with prize ribbons?
   Yes / No

10. Is there a Pegasus?
    Yes / No

11. Is there a picture of a silver fish in the area?
    Yes / No

12. Is there a picture of a hammer in the area?
    Yes / No

13. Is there a picture of a paint brush?
    Yes / No

14. Is there a jester's hat?
    Yes / No

15. Does one of the horses appear to be sleeping?
    Yes / No

16. Collection Time! If you run out of things to find on the Carrousel, this might be a good time to work on your Collections. If you haven't started one yet, see page 13 for suggestions.

Mad Tea Party

1. Mad Tea Party has many beautiful lights. What are the lights shaped as?
    a. Lanterns and tulips
    b. Lanterns and hearts
    c. Lanterns and roses
    d. Lanterns and clock faces

2. Where can you find the fraction 10/6?
    a. On the height requirement sign; you must be 10/6.
    b. On the Mad Hatter's straw-roofed house. Check the address.
    c. On the Mad Hatter's hat on the ride's sign.
    d. What is 10/6? There's no such thing.

3. Have a look at the teacups. How many teacups are unadorned?

    a. 6
    b. 9
    c. 11
    d. 7

4. Now look at the whirling twirling floor beneath the teacups. Think about the characters in *Alice in Wonderland*. What character from the story is represented in the colors of the floor?

    a. Queen of Hearts
    b. The Cheshire Cat
    c. Alice
    d. The Mad Hatter

5. How good are you at counting moving objects? Try to count the teacups. How many are there in all?

    a. 20
    b. 16
    c. 18
    d. 22

6. Check the teacups again. Check off all of the designs you see.

    ❑   Heart
    ❑   Daisy
    ❑   Spade
    ❑   Club
    ❑   Diamond
    ❑   Tulip

7. Collection Time! If you are still waiting to be invited to the tea party, this is a great time to work on a Collection or two. See page 13 if you need ideas for things to collect.

Matterhorn Bobsleds

1. From the queue to get on the Matterhorn, find and check off each ride you can see.
- ❑ Alice in Wonderland
- ❑ Finding Nemo Submarine Voyage
- ❑ Autopia
- ❑ "it's a small world"
- ❑ Mad Tea Party
- ❑ Pinocchio's Daring Journey
- ❑ Dumbo the Flying Elephant
- ❑ Space Mountain
- ❑ King Arthur Carrousel
- ❑ Snow White's Scary Adventures

2. What can be found on top of the chalet?
   a. A weather vane with a sled on it
   b. Three chimneys
   c. A red pennant
   d. A bird's nest

3. Can you find stained glass?
   Yes / No

4. As you wait in line, you will come to many crests and signs. Cross off each of the images listed below that you can find in a crest or a sign.
- ❑ Three birds with freckles
- ❑ A small white and red picture of Sleeping Beauty Castle
- ❑ A bluish-purple flower
- ❑ Two small houses
- ❑ Five stars that are two colors each
- ❑ A red triangle
- ❑ The word "bobsleds"
- ❑ The capital letters "V R"

- ❑ A very long horn
- ❑ A red cross
- ❑ A sled with an axe behind it
- ❑ An eagle peeking out from behind a key
- ❑ Shoes with buckles
- ❑ A beast who looks like he is about to be sick
- ❑ A yellow sun
- ❑ A goat
- ❑ A man with a staff

5. Collection Time! If you are still waiting for your bobsled ride, this is a great time to work on a Collection or two.

Mr. Toad's Wild Ride

Queue Entry
1. What does Mr. Toad have in his hand as you enter the queue?

a. A lollipop   b. A cane

c. A key   d. A monocle

2. What is unusual about the chimney on the building that houses Mr. Toad's ride?

a. It has carvings of Mr. Toad's head.

b. It has real smoke coming out of it.

c. It has a car and road carved into it.

d. All of the above

Stone Shields
3. There are four stone shields with Mr. Toad characters carved on them. Which of the following characters is not carved on a shield?

a. J. Thaddeus Toad, ESQ.

b. Angus Macbadger

    c. Mr. Mole
    d. Mr. Rat
    e. Perry the Platypus
    f. All of these characters are carved on
      shields.

4. Which character is wearing glasses?
    a. J. Thaddeus Toad, ESQ.
    b. Mr. Rat
    c. Mr. Mole
    d. Angus Macbadger

5. Which character is wearing a jaunty little cravat? (A cravat is a fancy necktie.)
    a. Mr. Rat
    b. J. Thaddeus Toad, ESQ.
    c. Mr. Mole
    d. Angus Macbadger

6. Who tries to cure Toad's "motormania"?
    a. J. Thaddeus Toad, ESQ. himself
    b. Mr. Rat   c. Mr. Mole
    d. Angus Macbadger   e. All of the above

7. Who is wearing a bow tie?
    a. Angus Macbadger
    b. Mr. Mole
    c. Mr. Rat
    d. J. Thaddeus Toad, ESQ.

After the Stone Shields

8. "Ho ho," what must you do to know what driving really is?
    a. Sit still   b. Listen well
    c. Be fearless   d. Jump like a frog

9. Where are you going on the wild ride?
    a. Fishing   b. To the country
    c. To the store   d. Nowhere in
                              particular

10. If you look around very carefully you may find a picture of Mr. Toad driving something other than a car. What other vehicle is Mr. Toad driving?

    a. A horse and buggy   b. A bicycle

    c. A tricycle   d. A train

    e. All of the above—that frog loves to drive!

Inside Queue

11. In the queue area indoors you'll see carved wooden toad heads wearing crowns. How many are there?

    a. 8   b. 4

    c. 6   d. 10

12. Mr. Toad has many interesting knickknacks. Which of these knickknacks is not in Mr. Toad's library area?

    a. A stained-glass frog lamp

    b. A judge's gavel

    c. A shiny black glass frog

    d. A sailing ship

13. Treasure Hunt Time! Have a look at the mural. See how many of the following items you can find before you climb behind the wheel of your car. Hey, do you have a driver's license?

- ❑ A "slow" sign
- ❑ Buckteeth
- ❑ A handlebar mustache
- ❑ Someone peeking out of the door
- ❑ Someone behind bars
- ❑ A bicycle
- ❑ The Tower Bridge
- ❑ Someone wearing pink
- ❑ Someone about to fall in the water
- ❑ A life preserver
- ❑ An inn
- ❑ Three barrels

Peter Pan's Flight

Queue Entry

1. You will come to a glass window. Have a look inside. Which of the following items is not in the window?

    a. Pirates' booty in a chalice

    b. A jewel

    c. A star

    d. A pirate's eye patch

2. Look at the wide main entrance to Sleeping Beauty Castle. Over it you will see three shields. Each of them is decorated with several pictures in groups of three. Which of the following is not pictured in triplicate on the shields?

    a. Crows

    b. Stars

    c. Beasts

    d. All of the above are pictured in groups of three.

3. Looking away from the ride itself into Fantasyland, can you find a knight on a horse?

    Yes / No

4. There are two weather vanes topping the Peter Pan's Flight building. What is featured on them?

    a. A fairy and Peter

    b. A boat and a crocodile

    c. Peter and a boat

    d. A pirate flag and flying children

5. Can you find a place where many carved hearts and circles are close together?
     a. On the railing
     b. On the walls
     c. On the window shutters
     d. On the rooftops

6. What is hanging from a hook?
     a. A pirate's map   b. A lantern
     c. A bucket   d. A cage

Mural and Audio Questions

7. Which famous London landmark is not present in the mural?
     a. London Bridge (a bridge with many arches)
     b. Big Ben (a large clock tower)
     c. Tower Bridge (a bridge with a tower on either side)
     d. Buckingham Palace (a huge rectangular white palace)

8. What things from home are the Darling children taking with them?
     a. A teddy bear   b. An umbrella
     c. A storybook   d. Both 'a' and 'b'
     e. Both 'b' and 'c'

9. What do you need to be on your way?
     a. A fairy   b. A map
     c. A touch of pixie dust
     d. Both 'a' and 'c'

10. Treasure Hunt Time! See how much pirate booty you can dig up before it is time to fly out of the nursery windows. Good luck there, matey.
     ❑ Four skulls
     ❑ A harp
     ❑ Two cannons
     ❑ Someone with his tongue hanging out
     ❑ A totem pole

- ❏ A telescope
- ❏ A wrecked ship
- ❏ Three crow's-nests
- ❏ A top hat
- ❏ A rope being used for no good
- ❏ A waterfall
- ❏ Someone wearing glasses
- ❏ Someone taking a nap
- ❏ Two hats with feathers in them
- ❏ The end of the rainbow

Pinocchio's Daring Journey

Queue Entry

1. The windows are stained glass. Which color is not in the windows?

    a. Dark blue   b. Light blue

    c. Red   d. Green

2. How many candles are in the chandelier?

    a. 8   b. 6

    c. 5   d. 10

3. What is the name of the puppeteer featured on the poster?

    a. Mr. Mistoffelees

    b. Sinbad the Magnificent

    c. The Great Stromboli

    d. Jiminy Cricket

4. Look around for a ledge. What or who is perched on it?

    a. A flowerpot

    b. Jiminy Cricket

    c. The Blue Fairy

    d. A toy puppet

Mural Questions

5. What is the name of the island where the boys are being sent?
   a. The Forbidden Island
   b. The Island of Lost Toys
   c. Carnival Island
   d. Pleasure Island

6. Who is in the Pinocchio mural?
   a. Pinocchio   b. The cat
   c. The fox   d. Jiminy Cricket
   e. All of the above

7. How many boys can be seen on the stagecoach?
   a. 6   b. 8
   c. 7   d. 5

8. What naughty activities are the boys on the coach participating in?
   a. Shooting a slingshot
   b. Smoking a cigar
   c. Punching each other
   d. All of the above
   e. Only 'a' and 'b'

9. Treasure Hunt Time! Look at the mural. See if you can find all of the following items, no strings attached.
   - A bottle of milk
   - A hot air balloon
   - Two books
   - Two bags of coins
   - An apple
   - A flowerpot
   - A cork
   - A crescent moon
   - A ripped glove
   - Three feathers
   - A horn
   - A mallet

- ❏ A cane
- ❏ A barrel
- ❏ A Ferris wheel

Snow White's Scary Adventures

1. Treasure Hunt Time! Try to find the following treasures as you wait. Some of these treasures belong in the woods and some in the wicked queen's castle, but they all belong on your list.

- ❏ Stone squirrels with very strong tails
- ❏ The evil queen's crown all lit up
- ❏ Stone bunnies
- ❏ Stone flowers
- ❏ Rubies
- ❏ Evil's Delight
- ❏ A door knocker
- ❏ A heart with a dagger through it
- ❏ A crow perched on a skull
- ❏ An apple you should never eat
- ❏ Owl faces peeking at you

2. Extra Points!!! Earn 5 bonus points if you see the evil queen peek at you before you get on the ride.

3. Collection Time! If you are still waiting to enter Snow White's forest, this is a great time to work on a Collection or two. See page 13 if you need ideas for a new Collection.

Storybook Land Canal Boats

1. On what building is the sign for Storybook Land painted?
   a. A castle
   b. A house made of sticks
   c. A lighthouse
   d. A bridge

2. Listen carefully. What sounds from other rides can you hear while you wait to board your boat? Earn 1 point for each ride you can check off.
   ❑ People screaming on the teacups
   ❑ The "toot toot" of the "Casey Jr." train
   ❑ The waterfalls on the Matterhorn
   ❑ A fourth ride (name the ride and the sound)

3. Look up at the pretty garden. The flowers are giving you a message. What are they saying?
   a. Read a Book   b. Storybook Land
   c. Mickey Mouse   d. Disneyland

4. Watch out, someone seems to be eating up the boats. Who is having a snack?
   a. The big bad wolf   b. A dragon
   c. A giant baby   d. A great whale

5. Look around for flags blowing in the wind. What color are they?
   a. Pink   b. Purple
   c. Orange   d. Silver

6. Collection Time! If you are still waiting to board your boat, this is a great time to work on your Collections.

Fantasyland Answers

Alice in Wonderland
1) d. All of the above
2) b. 10/6 (10 shillings sixpence in old English money)
3) c. Nobody
4) b. Leaves
5) a. The Caterpillar
6) b. Flowers
7) Total Treasures found _____

Casey Jr. Circus Train
1) Total Treasures found _____
2) a. Three times and then it arrives at the station. (Give
   yourself 5 bonus points if you got this right.)
3) Number of items collected _____

Dumbo the Flying Elephant
1) Total Treasures found _____
2) b. A feather – and 3 bonus points
3) Number of items collected _____

"it's a small world"
1) b. 4/22/64
2) d. Dog
3) Yes; it's an hourglass.
4) c. Flowers
5) a. & d. The Leaning Tower of Pisa & the Eiffel Tower
6) c. Disneyland Railroad
7) Total Pinwheels found _____
8) Total Treasures found _____
Clock Parade Pop Quiz
9) Yes
10) No
11) Yes
12) No
13) Yes
14) Yes
15) No

"it's a small world", cont'd.

16) Yes
17) No
18) No
19) Yes
20) Yes
21) Yes
22) Yes
23) Yes
24) No
25) Yes
26) Yes
27) No
28) Yes
29) Yes
30) No
31) Yes
32) Yes
33) Yes
34) Yes

King Arthur Carrousel

1) c. Sleeping Beauty
2) d. A crown
3) No
4) Yes
5) Yes
6) Yes
7) Yes
8) No
9) Yes
10) No (Pegasus is a flying horse.)
11) Yes
12) Yes
13) Yes
14) Yes
15) No
16) Number of items collected _____

Mad Tea Party

1) a. Lanterns and tulips
2) c. On the Mad Hatter's hat on the ride's sign

3) b. 9
4) b. The Cheshire Cat
5) c. 18
6) Find all six designs to earn 1 point
7) Number of items collected _____

Matterhorn Bobsleds

1) Total Rides sighted _____
2) c. A red pennant
3) Yes
4) Total Images found _____
5) Number of items collected _____

Mr. Toad's Wild Ride

1) d. A monocle
2) a. It has carvings of Mr. Toad's head.
Stone Shields
3) e. Perry the Platypus
4) d. Angus Macbadger
5) c. Mr. Mole
6) b. Mr. Rat
7) d. J. Thaddeus Toad, ESQ.
After the Stone Shields
8) a. Sit still
9) d. Nowhere in particular
10) a. A horse and buggy
Inside Queue
11) c. 6
12) b. A judge's gavel
13) Total Treasures found _____

Peter Pan's Flight

1) d. A pirate's eye patch
2) c. Beasts
3) Yes
4) b. A boat and a crocodile
5) a. On the railing
6) b. A lantern
Mural and Audio Questions
7) d. Buckingham Palace
8) a. A teddy bear
9) c. A touch of pixie dust

Peter Pan's Flight, cont'd.
10) Total Treasures found _____

Pinocchio's Daring Journey
1) d. Green
2) b. 6
3) c. The Great Stromboli
4) a. A flowerpot
Mural Questions
5) d. Pleasure Island
6) e. All of the above
7) c. 7
8) e. Only 'a' and 'b'
9) Total Treasures found _____

Snow White's Scary Adventures
1) Total Treasures found _____
2) Add 5 bonus points if the queen peeked at you
3) Number of items collected _____

Storybook Land Canal Boats
1) c. A lighthouse
2) Total Rides heard _____
3) b. Storybook Land
4) d. A great whale
5) a. Pink
6) Number of items collected _____

Mickey's Toontown

Toontown Scavenger Hunt

Welcome to Mickey's Toontown. While you visit this great town, you'll find treasures everywhere. Some are easy to find and some will take careful scavenging, but I am sure that you are up to it. This scavenger hunt will take you all through the town. If you are ready to be a treasure hunter, then here we go.

1. Find the two huge letters on the gates to Toontown. What are they?
   a. M and T
   b. D and L
   c. M and M
   d. W and D

2. Can you find Landmark 3½? What are the rules found there?
   a. Do not walk on your feet, hands only.
   b. Absolutely NO erasers allowed.
   c. You must wear Mickey Mouse ears.
   d. Please play safely.

3. What's the Motto of Toontown?
   a. Eat, Drink and Be Silly
   b. Draw, Baby, Draw
   c. Laughter Is Sunshine You Can Hear
   d. Have Fun

Roger Rabbit Area

4. Find four fish spitting. What are they riding on?

    a. Old tires   b. Horses

    c. A windmill   d. Motorcycles

5. Can you find a license plate reading RRabbt?
    Yes / No

Downtown Streets

6. Find the insurance company. What injuries does it cover?

    a. Hotfoots

    b. Getting Hit On The Head

    c. Falling Anvils, Safes, And Pianos

    d. Smashing Into Brick Walls Disguised As Tunnels

    e. All of the above

    f. None of the above; they went out of business

7. Find a doorbell at the insurance company. What happens when you push it?

    a. The doorbell sneezes.

    b. A light comes on inside the insurance building.

    c. Crashing sounds

    d. The bell asks you to stop pushing it.

8. Can you find a falling safe zone?
    Yes / No

9. Whose byline is "Slow and Steady Solves the Case"?

    a. Toby the Tortoise Detective Agency

    b. Goofy's Private Eye Agency

    c. Pluto's Sniff-It-Out Dog Training

    d. Donald's Duck-the-Cops Police Station

10. Visit the warehouse area where all the crates are stored. Can you find the crate that "moos"?
    Yes / No

11. Find the Fireworks factory. Can you make an explosion happen?
    Yes / No

12. Can you find the cat's meow?
    Yes / No

13. Can you find breaking glass?
    Yes / No

14. Can you find a warning for "Gags Ahead"?
    Yes / No

15. Find a streetlamp that is not quite right. What is strange about it?
    a. It is lit by fireflies.
    b. It is twisted.
    c. It is upside-down.
    d. Chip 'n Dale are trapped inside.

16. Can you find the Gym? Who is the proprietor?
    a. Goofy   b. Roger Rabbit
    c. Daisy Duck   d. Horace Horsecollar

17. What is absolutely, positively, unquestionably forbidden, unless you really feel like it?
    a. Walking on the grass
    b. Patting your head while rubbing your tummy
    c. Opening the door to the power house
    d. Lifting the dumbbell

18. Who is Toontown's dentist?
    a. Dr. Drillum   b. Dr. Lollypop
    c. Dr. Toothless   d. Dr. Smiley

19. What happens when you ring the bell at the camera shop?
- a. The door locks and the windows shut.
- b. It takes your picture.
- c. It tells you to say "Cheese."
- d. An eye appears in the peep hole.

20. Can you find a wacky street sign?
Yes / No

21. What sort of property is operated by the Three Little Pigs?
- a. Chinny Chin Chin Construction Company
- b. The Bricklayers Association
- c. Straw Bales R Us Horse Feed and Care
- d. Pig Brothers Rustic Stick Furniture

22. What sort of property is operated by the Big Bad Wolf?
- a. Huffin & Puffin Wrecking Company
- b. BBW Pit Barbeque
- c. BB Wolf Chimney Sweeps
- d. None; Mr. Wolf is retired.

23. What happens when you try to mail something?
- a. The mailbox burps.
- b. The mailbox refuses to open.
- c. The mailbox insults you.
- d. The mailbox tries to eat your hand.

24. What is to be found at Professor Ludwig von Drake's Old Curiosity Shop?
- a. Decoy ducks looking for a good home
- b. Curiosity Shakes: Shake it, Drink it & You're Curious Again.
- c. All De Tings You Vant
- d. Lots of assorted Toons who wonder about you

25. Can you find a place where it will be safe for a cooked chicken to cross the road?
    Yes / No

26. Can you spot a sign made by a signmaker who needs to return to school? What is it?
    a. The Toontown Library
    b. The Toontown School
    c. The Toontown mayor's office
    d. The Toontown doctor's office

27. Who is allowed to visit the Toontown Library?
    a. Toons only   b. Books only
    c. No one at all, keep out.
    d. Cast Members only

28. Where can you find a bell that probably has a bad headache?
    a. On the clock tower
    b. On the school building
    c. In the town square
    d. Over the entrance to the gas station

29. In what building does Scrooge McDuck work?
    a. At the bank, as the head of the security guards
    b. At the police station, as the fines collector
    c. At the courthouse, as an investment counselor
    d. At the gas station, as the owner and price setter

30. What building proudly displays its official seal over the front door?
    a. The courthouse
    b. The bank
    c. The fireworks makers
    d. The Toontown Insurance Company

31. What sign badly needs reconstruction?
    a. Construction Company
    b. Dog Pound
    c. City Hall
    d. Dept. of Street Repair

32. What is for sale at Pluto's Dog House?
    a. Stuffed pets
    b. Hot dogs
    c. Pins
    d. Your own Toon dog collar

33. What is available at the bank in case of emergency?
    a. A fire extinguisher
    b. An exit
    c. A small hammer
    d. A siren

34. What sign is held up by a paintbrush?
    a. The entrance to Roger Rabbit's Cartoon Spin
    b. Toontown Museum of Art
    c. Daisy Duck's Art Studio
    d. The Dept. of Ink & Paint

35. What kinds of water are served at Goofy's Water?
    a. Surfin' Water   b. Loopy Water
    c. Wet Water   d. Zippy Water
    e. All of the above

36. Does anything happen when you drink the water?
    Yes / No

37. What is free at the gas station?
    a. Popcorn   b. Bubbles
    c. Air   d. Band-Aids

38. What two types of gas are available for purchase at Goofy's Gas Station?
    a. Slow and Fast
    b. Maple syrup and Chocolate sauce
    c. Going and Gone
    d. Ka-Boom and Regular

39. What is unique about the gas tanks at Toontown?
    a. They are not advised for cars.
    b. They have fish living in them.
    c. They contain rainbow-colored gas.
    d. There are no gas hoses.

40. What is the motto of Goofy's Gas Station?
    a. "If we can't fix it, we won't."
    b. "Every day is a good day at Goofy's."
    c. "See us for a TOON up."
    d. "Never drive without tires."

41. What is on sale at Goofy's Gas Station?
    a. There is half off for a "Car Toon-Up."
    b. Mood adjustment for grumpy cars
    c. Goodtoon Tires
    d. Safety parachutes

42. Can you find a place where a wrong turn is OK?
    Yes / No

Suburban Streets
43. What is on Mickey's license plate?
    a. TOPMOUSE   b. MICKEY 1
    c. MMLOVMM   d. STEAMBOATW

44. Can you find Mickey holding a conductor's baton?
    Yes / No

45. What is special about the flag on Minnie's mailbox?
   a. The flag is shaped like a ribbon.
   b. The flag goes down not up.
   c. It is polka-dotted like her dress.
   d. If you touch the flag it giggles like you tickled it.

46. What shape is the weather vane on Minnie's house?
   a. Flower
   b. Heart with arrow
   c. Two mouse faces kissing
   d. A teapot

47. Who has a wishing well?
   a. Jessica Rabbit
   b. Daisy Duck
   c. The wishing well is in the center of town and belongs to everyone.
   d. Minnie Mouse

48. What shape cutout is on the shutters to Minnie's house?
   a. Heart   b. Flower
   c. Mouse head   d. Bow

49. Can you find Mickey Mouse dressed up like Cupid?
   Yes / No

50. Who has a sign for Toontown in the backyard?
   a. Goofy   b. Donald
   c. Chip 'n Dale   d. Mickey

51 Can you find something missing from the tree where Chip 'n Dale live? If yes, what?
   Yes / No

52. Where can you find Chip 'n Dale playing with acorns?
    a. On the very top of the tree
    b. Peeking from a window
    c. On the sign
    d. Sliding on the roof

53. What two things are on Chip 'n Dale's mailbox?
    a. Two chipmunks
    b. An acorn and an autumn leaf
    c. A piece of mail and an acorn
    d. What mailbox?

54. Who is prominently featured on the front of Donald's boat?
    a. The Little Mermaid b. Daisy Duck
    c. Mickey Mouse   d. Tinker Bell

55. Can you find Donald's missing shirt and hat?
Yes / No

56. Why would it be difficult to deliver mail to Donald Duck?
    a. His mailbox is locked.
    b. His mailbox is on the very top of the boat.
    c. His mailbox is underwater.
    d. His mailbox is floating.

57. What is the name of Donald's boat?
    a. SS Miss Daisy   b. SS Mine all Mine
    c. SS Toontown   d. SS Quack

58. When you visit Goofy's house, check out his outside lighting. Which of these things is used as part of the porch lighting at Goofy's?
    a. Jelly Bean Jar   b. Fish Jelly Jar
    c. Grape Jelly Jar   d. Both 'a' and 'b'
    e. All of the above

59. Goofy is using some things in unusual ways at his house. See if you can locate the following things that are being used in a Goofy way:

- ❑ A bucket
- ❑ A baby's cradle
- ❑ An oar
- ❑ A pot
- ❑ A very big hat
- ❑ A gavel
- ❑ A chimney

60. What is the matter with Goofy's car?
   a. All of the tires are flat.
   b. All of the tires are patched.
   c. It seems to have been in a collision with his mailbox.
   d. All of the above

61. What color is Goofy's laundry basket?
   a. Red   b. Blue
   c. Green   d. Rainbow

62. Goofy has a garden. Find his scarecrow. What does it resemble?
   a. Mickey Mouse
   b. A big crow wearing a hat
   c. A normal scarecrow
   d. Goofy himself

63. Can you find someone who is not frightened by the scarecrow?
   Yes / No

64. What foods are growing in the garden?
   a. Popcorn   b. Apples
   c. Watermelons   d. Both 'a' and 'c'
   e. Both 'b' and 'c'

Disneyland Railroad Station

1. Treasure Hunt Time! See how many Toon treasures you can find before it is time to catch your train.

- ❏ A copper lantern
- ❏ A big crown
- ❏ A moon
- ❏ Something that is spinning
- ❏ A piece of luggage just right for Pluto
- ❏ A piece of luggage perfect for Minnie Mouse
- ❏ A water tower
- ❏ An aqua-colored barrel
- ❏ A pulley
- ❏ A picture of Mickey Mouse, or at least his head
- ❏ The word "Forecast"

2. Extra Points!!! For 10 bonus points solve this riddle: "Find a train that always stays here, but could go in any direction it wished."

Gadget's Go Coaster

Queue Entry

1. Gadget's Go Coaster is presented by:
    a. Dole   b. Sparkle
    c. Bank of America   d. Mickey Mouse

2. What tool is not on the Gadget's Go Coaster sign?
    a. A wrench   b. A magnet
    c. A ruler   d. A hammer

3. Look at Gadget's house. Which of the following is ingeniously used as a pillar to hold up the patio cover?
    a. A stack of acorns b. A flute
    c. A magnifying glass d. A pencil

4. The drainpipes on the house are striped to look like what?
    a. The Cheshire Cat b. An American flag
    c. A candy cane   d. A rainbow

5. Check the windows on Gadget's house. What can you find sticking out of a window that shouldn't be there?
    a. A bird's nest   b. A mailbox
    c. A tree branch   d. A hose

The Gadget

6. The motor running Gadget's coaster is made of many unique parts. Which of the following "parts" is not on the motor?
    a. A Slinky   b. Some Tinkertoys
    c. Some bottle caps d. A teacup

7. What can of soup is featured on the motor?
   a. Hickory
   b. Acorn
   c. Peanut
   d. Chestnut

8. What words are on the gears of the gadget?
   a. Fizz
   b. Zing
   c. Zip
   d. All of the above
   e. All but 'b'

9. There is a fish tank on the gadget. What is it resting on?
   a. A globe
   b. A racing flag
   c. An upside-down stool
   d. A deflated soccer ball

End of the Queue

10. Have a look at the weather vane on Gadget's house. North, South, East, and West all have a shape around them. What is it?
   a. An acorn
   b. A mouse head
   c. A fish
   d. Gears

11. Gadget's mailbox has her title on it. What is Gadget's title?
   a. Mad Scientist
   b. Inventor
   c. Doctor
   d. Collector Extraordinaire

12. To ride Gadget's Go Coaster you must be 35 inches tall. What is this measurement taken on?
   a. A giant ruler
   b. A giant acorn
   c. A giant pencil
   d. A giant Tinkertoy

13. Treasure Hunt Time! You are almost there. Can you find these last few things before you climb aboard?
   ❑   A compass
   ❑   Dominos
   ❑   A ruler
   ❑   A thimble

- ❏ A diagram showing how the Go Coaster's motor should be made
- ❏ A jack
- ❏ Acorn lamps

Roger Rabbit's Car Toon Spin

Queue Entry

1. When you enter the line for Roger Rabbit, what is the speed limit?

a. 25 mph   b. 40 mph

c. 50 mph   d. 65 mph

2. Can you find a sign that is confusing?

Yes / No

3. There is a crate containing rearview mirrors. What is unusual about it?

a. The writing is reversed like a reflection.

b. The writing appears farther away than it really is.

c. All the mirrors are broken and a label shows how many years' bad luck are in the crate.

d. They all look like sideview mirrors.

4. Treasure Hunt Time! It is time for a quick hunt. Can you locate:

- ❏ Two steering wheels
- ❏ A deflated tire
- ❏ Two hubcaps
- ❏ A wrench
- ❏ Several nuts and bolts

5. Find a street sign. What street have you come to?

    a. Jessica Rabbit Lane   b. 2nd Avenue
    c. Alley Street   d. Roger Rabbit Road

6. When you arrive in the loading area, look around. Where does the crate need to be delivered?

    a. To J Rabbit's Dressing Room
    b. To Toon's Auto Paint and Body Shop
    c. To the Gag Factory
    d. To the Ink & Paint Club

7. There is a pipe that has been repaired. What was used to fix the pipe?

    a. Quack brand duck tape
    b. Lots of sticky glue
    c. A Band-Aid
    d. A polka-dot bandana
    e. All of the above; that thing is really stuck now.

8. There was a turtle. What was his name?

    a. Trevor   b. Todd
    c. Toby   d. Tanker

Ink & Paint Club

9. When you come to the Ink & Paint Club, you can see a silhouette in the window. Whose silhouette is there?

    a. Jessica Rabbit   b. Roger Rabbit
    c. Baby Herman   d. Mickey Mouse

10. The bouncer will come to the door of the Ink & Paint Club. What does he tell you to do if you have no password?

    a. "Come back when you have it."
    b. "Amscray."
    c. "Take it up with the management."
    d. "Get lost, coppers."

11. Can you find a silver brick wall that is breaking?

Yes / No

12. Who is going to perform the "Hungarian Rhapsody"?

a. Donald   b. Jessica Rabbit

c. Baby Herman   d. Roger Rabbit

13. Can you find Jessica Rabbit's Dressing Room?

Yes / No

Prop Cage Area

14. You have come to the prop cage. It is filled with many wonderful props for Toons to use. See if you can locate the following props:

- ❑ Coconut cream pies
- ❑ A crown
- ❑ A wilted star
- ❑ A damaged drum
- ❑ A polka-dot tie
- ❑ A chandelier
- ❑ A pink handbag
- ❑ A hooked fish
- ❑ An umbrella with a snake-head handle
- ❑ A cowboy hat with arrows
- ❑ A vase with flowers
- ❑ A sword

15. What has Dumbo lost?

a. Timothy Mouse

b. His way; he needs directions.

c. A magic feather

d. Dumbo? What ride are you on?

16. There is an audition on Tuesday for "Melody Time." Who should not show up?

a. Live actors   b. Any animals

c. Giants   d. Both 'a' and 'c'

17. Where is the exit?
    a. Stage left
    b. Stage right
    c. Through the Ink & Paint Club
    d. On the roof

18. What should you remember if you want to Get Hip – Don't Get "The Dip"?
    a. Weasels are on the loose.
    b. Don't go out alone after dark.
    c. Go out in pairs.
    d. Those all sound important to me.

19. Why should we keep out?
    a. Cast Members only
    b. Wet paint
    c. Known weasel hangout
    d. Falling pianos

The Baby's Room
20. Can you find a baby with something he definitely should not have? What is it?
    a. A gun
    b. A bottle marked "poison"
    c. A weasel by the tail
    d. A cigar

21. What is the baby reading?
    a. "Winnie the Pooh"
    b. A script for "Melody Time"
    c. "Toon Racing Form"
    d. The baby is sleeping.

22. The baby's room has a clock in it. Who is the clock maker?
    a. Mickey Watches
    b. White Rabbit's Time Co.
    c. Toon Time Co.
    d. Time To Go Clock Co.

23. What is unusual about the clock?
  a. It is upside down.
  b. It has no numbers.
  c. It is running in the wrong direction.
  d. Its hands are actually hands.

24. What does Baby Herman appear to have been eating recently?
  a. A rather large sandwich
  b. A turkey leg
  c. French fries
  d. A birthday cake

25. Who or what is featured on Baby Herman's wallpaper?
  a. Mickey Mouse   b. Cigars
  c. Jessica Rabbit   d. Baby bottles

26. There is a calendar in Baby Herman's room. What month is it?
  a. January   b. August
  c. July   d. April

The Bad Neighborhood
27. Can you find the number 42?
  Yes / No

28. There is a sign that warns you to keep out. Whose silhouette appears above that sign?
  a. Jessica Rabbit   b. A weasel
  c. The bouncer   d. A police officer with
                            a club

29. What is in the olive drab barrels?
  a. Gasoline   b. Wacky Water
  c. Dip   d. A screaming sound;
                            keep it plugged.

30. What is not an ingredient in the "Dip"?
  a. Benzene   b. Turpentine
  c. Acetone   d. Neoprene

31. Can you find a pipe containing turpentine?
Yes / No

The End of the Line

32. What are the Cab Co. hours of operation?
    a. 8a.m.-4p.m.   b. 6a.m.-11p.m.
    c. 9a.m.-9p.m.   d. 7:30a.m.-7:30p.m.

33. What is located at "3 TIMESFAST ST. CANTSAY, IT"?
    a. Rubber Baby Buggy Bumpers Inc.
    b. Toy Boat, Toy Boat, Toy Boat &
       Picklepepper Inc.
    c. Woodchuck_&_Family_Woodcarvings.com
    d. She Sells Sea Shells Shell Shack

34. As you come to the area where you can see people starting on the ride, there is a large pile of car parts. There is not much time left until it is your turn. See how many of the following parts you can find before you climb into your car. **FP**

- ❑ A gauge pointing to red
- ❑ Two flat tires, one inside the other
- ❑ A wrench
- ❑ A gloved hand
- ❑ A streetlight
- ❑ A nut and bolt
- ❑ Three propellers
- ❑ A confusing street sign
- ❑ A steering wheel
- ❑ A dartboard
- ❑ A dollar bill

Mickey's Toontown Answers

Toontown Scavenger Hunt

1) a. M and T

2) d. Please play safely.

3) c. Laughter Is Sunshine You Can Hear

Roger Rabbit Area

4) a. Old tires

5) Yes

Downtown Streets

6) f. None of the above; they went out of business

7) c. Crashing sounds

8) Yes

9) a. Toby the Tortoise Detective Agency

10) Yes

11) Yes

12) Yes

13) Yes

14) Yes

15) b. It is twisted.

16) d. Horace Horsecollar

17) c. Opening the door to the power house

18) a. Dr. Drillum

19) b. It takes your picture.

20) Yes

21) a. Chinny Chin Chin Construction Company

22) d. None; Mr. Wolf is retired

23) c. The mailbox insults you.

24) c. All De Tings You Vant

25) Yes

26) b. The Toontown School

27) d. Cast Members only

28) a. On the clock tower

29) c. At the courthouse, as an investment counselor

30) a. The courthouse

31) d. Dept. of Street Repair

32) b. Hot dogs

33) c. A small hammer

34) d. The Dept of Ink & Paint

35) e. All of the above
36) Yes
37) c. Air
38) d. Ka-Boom and Regular
39) b. They have fish living in them.
40) a. "If we can't fix it, we won't."
41) c. Goodtoon Tires
42) Yes

Suburban Streets
43) b. MICKEY 1
44) Yes
45) c. It is polka-dotted like her dress
46) b. Heart with arrow
47) d. Minnie Mouse
48) a. Heart
49) Yes
50) d. Mickey
51) Yes, leaves
52) c. On the sign
53) b. An acorn and an autumn leaf
54) b. Daisy Duck
55) Yes
56) d. His mailbox is floating.
57) a. SS Miss Daisy
58) e. All of the above
59) Total Goofy uses found _____
60) d. All of the above
61) b. Blue
62) d. Goofy himself
63) Yes
64) d. Both 'a' & 'c'

Disneyland Railroad Station
1) Total Treasures found _____
2) The weather vane (Collect 10 bonus points if you solved this riddle.)

Gadget's Go Coaster
1) b. Sparkle
2) a. A wrench
3) d. A pencil
4) c. A candy cane

Gadget's Go Coaster, cont'd.
5) c. A tree branch
The Gadget
6) a. A Slinky
7) b. Acorn
8) e. All but 'b'
9) d. A deflated soccer ball
The End of the Queue
10) a. An acorn
11) b. Inventor
12) c. A giant pencil
13) Total Treasures found _____

Roger Rabbit's Car Toon Spin
1) b. 40 mph
2) Yes
3) a. The writing is reversed like a reflection.
4) Total Treasures found _____
5) c. Alley Street
6) d. To the Ink & Paint Club
7) d. A polka-dot bandana
8) c. Toby
Ink & Paint Club
9) a. Jessica Rabbit
10) b. "Amscray."
11) Yes
12) a. Donald
13) Yes
Prop Cage Area
14) Total Props found _____
15) c. A magic feather
16) d. Both 'a' and 'c'
17) a. Stage left
18) d. Those are all important to me.
19) b. Wet paint
The Baby's Room
20) d. A cigar
21) c. "Toon Racing Form"
22) c. Toon Time Co.
23) d. Its hands are actually hands.
24) a. A rather large sandwich

25) c. Jessica Rabbit
26) b. August

The Bad Neighborhood

27) Yes
28) b. A weasel
29) c. Dip
30) d. Neoprene
31) Yes

The End of the Line

32) a. 8a.m.–4p.m.
33) b. Toy Boat, Toy Boat, Toy Boat & Picklepepper Inc.
34) Total Listed Parts found _____

New Orleans Square

Disneyland Railroad Station

1. Treasure Hunt Time! See how many treasures you can spot before your train departs.

- ☐ The French Market
- ☐ A water tower
- ☐ A fountain
- ☐ A different form of communication (Listen closely!)
- ☐ A place to buy imports
- ☐ Someone's white shirt getting dry
- ☐ A sign with a pointing hand
- ☐ A red axe
- ☐ Four things that are for fire use only
- ☐ The large initials D. R. R.
- ☐ A ladder

2. Extra points!!! For 4 bonus points, find a poster of the Disneyland Railroad. What station stop is not mentioned?

a. Frontierland

b. Toontown

c. Tomorrowland

d. Main Street, U.S.A.

3. Collection Time! If you are still waiting to board your train, why not work on a Collection or two? Add to one you've started or choose a new one from the Collection ideas on page 13. (Tip: Pirate flags or kids dressed as pirates would work especially well here.)

Haunted Mansion

Queue Entry

1. Who is accepting reservations?
   a. 999 Ghouls and Ghosts
   b. I. M. Mortal
   c. The Ghost Relations Department
   d. Rustin Peece

2. Who is dying to meet you?
   a. 999 Ghouls and Ghosts
   b. The Grim Reaper
   c. B. Yond
   d. I. Trudy Departed

The Pet Cemetery

3. Who is our friend until the end?
   a. Old Flybait   b. Buddy
   c. U. R. Gone   d. Rupert

4. Who croaked on August 9, 1869?
   a. Old Flybait   b. Freddie
   c. Levi Tation   d. Web Foot

5. Whose epitaph is partly upside down?
   a. Lilac
   b. Ray N. Carnation
   c. Freddie
   d. Up C. Daisy

6. Can you find a sailboat that can travel in any direction?

Yes / No

7. What is unusual about the grave marking for FiFi?

a. It is located in the crypt for people and should have been in the pet cemetery.

b. It is located in the pet cemetery and belonged in the human crypt.

c. It is painted.

d. It is made from her favorite treat.

8. How did Jeb die?

a. He fell from a very high height.

b. He was eaten by a cat.

c. He was hit on the head by a garden rake.

d. He got tangled up in a spider's web.

9. In the queue-area pet cemetery, only one of the following has an epitaph on its stone. Which is it?

a. Squirrel   b. Rabbit

c. Rat   d. Cat

10. Who died on October 10, 1867?

a. Fish   b. Up C. Daisy

c. Frog   d. Ray N. Carnation

11. Who was short on common sense?

a. Up C. Daisy

b. Lilac

c. Ray N. Carnation

d. Rosie

12. Whose fatal mistake was frightening the gardener?

a. Spider   b. Dog

c. Skunk   d. Snake

The Human Crypt

13. How many urns on brick columns can be seen around the mansion?

a. 10   b. 13

c. 14   d. 17

14. Who is not resting in peace in the human crypt?

a. B. Yond   b. U. R. Gone

c. Levi Tation   d. M. T. Tomb

15. Read the names in the human crypt carefully. They are clever plays on words. How many can you decipher? _____

Pirates of the Caribbean

The Outside Queue Area

1. As ye enter the world of pirates there will be a warning for ye, matey. What is it?

a. You may get wet.

b. You may have your treasure stolen.

c. You will meet pirates; be warned.

d. You must be at least 42 inches tall to take this ride.

e. All of the above

2. As you enter, there are two large trees with lights hanging from them. How many lights are in the trees?

a. 10

b. 11

c. 14

d. 16

3. Above ye heads there be a very fancy railing. It be green. In the railing made of pirates' gold there are initials to be found. What two sets of initials appear in gold?

    a. CD and MD

    b. WD and RD

    c. MM and WD

    d. MP and KP

4. There is a door with an address number on it. What is the number?

    a. 33

    b. 37

    c. 48

    d. 50

5. Can you find the correct words to finish this statement? "Sail with _____"

    a. the tide

    b. us, laddy; ye be a pirate

    c. Captain Jack Sparrow

    d. ye heart; follow ye map

The Inside Queue Area

6. There is a noisy parrot. What is he perched on?

    a. A gun   b. A skull

    c. A treasure chest   d. A shovel

7. Can you find an X that marks the spot?

    Yes / No

8. That parrot is trying to give you a message. Which of these things does the parrot tell you?

    a. Steady as she goes.

    b. Yo ho. Yo ho.

    c. Dead men tell no tales.

    d. Shiver me timbers.

    e. Pieces of eight, pieces of eight

    f. All of the above

    g. All but 'e'

9. Treasure Hunt Time! Have a look at the pirates' portraits. Locate as many of the following as you can before boarding your craft.

- ❏ A pirate missing a tooth
- ❏ A pair of binoculars
- ❏ Two rings
- ❏ An eagle
- ❏ A cane
- ❏ A pistol held to its owner by a sash
- ❏ A wine glass
- ❏ A beard divided in two
- ❏ A striped shirt
- ❏ A pistol tucked in a belt
- ❏ Furry sleeves
- ❏ A gold ear hoop

10. What is the name of the pier where you board your ship?

a. Sparrow Landing
b. New Orleans Dock
c. Blue Bayou Dock
d. None of the above

New Orleans Square Answers

Disneyland Railroad: New Orleans Square Station

1) Total Treasures found _____
2) b. Toontown (4 bonus points if you got this right.)
3) Number of items collected _____

Haunted Mansion

1) c. The Ghost Relations Department
2) a. 999 Ghouls and Ghosts

The Pet Cemetery

3) b. Buddy
4) a. Old Flybait
5) c. Freddie
6) Yes
7) d. It is made from her favorite treat.
8) d. He got tangled up in a spider's web.
9) c. Rat
10) a. Fish
11) b. Lilac
12) d. Snake

The Human Crypt

13) c. 14
14) a. B. Yond
15) Total Wordplays deciphered _____

Pirates of the Caribbean

1) a. You may get wet.
2) c. 14
3) b. WD and RD
4) d. 50
5) a. the tide

The Inside Queue Area

6) d. A shovel
7) Yes
8) f. All of the above
9) Total Treasures found _____
10) d. None of the above

Tomorrowland

Astro Orbitor

1. How many ships are there on the Astro Orbitor?

    a. 10   b. 11

    c. 12   d. 13

2. Look at the things around you both far and near. Can you find a window shaped like a cross?

    Yes / No

3. Look in the general direction of Sleeping Beauty Castle. Something occasionally flies into the air over there. What is it?

    a. A rocket ship   b. Water

    c. Tinker Bell   d. Glitter

4. You are standing near another Astro ride, Astro Blasters. What movie was it inspired by?

    a. *Monsters Inc.*   b. *Cars*

    c. *Star Wars*   d. *Toy Story 2*

5. When you get into your rocket ship, what will you need to do to make it go higher?

    a. Pull the controller back toward yourself.

    b. Push the controller away from yourself.

    c. Flap your arms like wings for better lift.

    d. Move the controller in a clockwise circle.

6. What will you do to lower your rocket ship?
   a. Push the controller away from yourself.
   b. Pull the controller toward yourself.
   c. Stop flapping.
   d. Move the controller in a counterclockwise circle.

7. The original version of Astro Orbitor opened in 1956. Is the Astro Orbitor older or younger than the oldest person in your group?
   Older / Younger

8. Is it older or younger than you?
   Older / Younger

9. Is the Astro Orbitor older or younger than your Grandma?
   Older / Younger

10. Collection Time! If you are still waiting to blast off, this is a great time to work on a Collection or two. If you want to start a new one, crazy backpacks, lightsabers, or planets should work well in Tomorrowland. Or think up one of your own. Need suggestions? Check page 13.

Autopia

1. What is the speed limit on the Autopia? **FP**
    a. As fast as you can
    b. 55 smiles per hour
    c. No faster than the car in front of you
    d. 25 miles per hour

2. What company presents the Autopia ride? **FP**
    a. Chevron   b. Bank of America
    c. Dole   d. Both 'b' and 'c'
    e. Both 'a' and 'c'

3. What shop can be seen across from the Autopia entrance? **FP**
    a. Fill Up Here   b. Goofy's Station
    c. The Drive Thru   d. Winner's Circle

4. Is there a Disneyland mailbox close by? **FP**
    Yes / No

5. How tall must you be to ride the Autopia alone? **FP**
    a. 52 inches   b. 54 inches
    c. 55 inches   d. 58 inches

6. What were the colors on the pennants you passed at the front of the ride? **FP**
    a. Red and blue   b. Black and white
    c. Blue and white   d. Red and white

7. What shouldn't you do once you hit the road? **FP**
    a. Hit the car in front of you
    b. Speed
    c. Drive offroad
    d. Back up

8. There is a car addressing you on a big screen. What is his name? **FP**
    a. Speedy
    b. Dusty
    c. Rusty
    d. Buddy

9. What is the delicious shake made from? **FP**
    a. High octane gas
    b. Pistons and bolts
    c. Motor oil
    d. Yuck, I don't want any please!

10. Who or what can you drive away according to the big screen outside? **FP**
    a. Your cares   b. Your parents
    c. Your time   d. Your friends

11. You've got to _____ positive? **FP**
    a. be
    b. drive to be
    c. always accept the
    d. accelerate the

12. - 13. Look at the license plates on the cars. While in line, try to find all of the letters A through Z and all of the numbers 1 through 9 on the plates. Cross them off as you find them and give yourself 1 point for each one you find. **FP**

12. A B C D E F G H I J K L M
     N O P Q R S T U V W X Y Z **FP**

13. 1 2 3 4 5 6 7 8 9 **FP**

14. How fast do the cars actually go when you put the pedal to the metal? **FP**
    a. 6.5 mph   b. 9.5 mph
    c. 10 mph   d. 15 mph

15. Why do the cars never stop? **FP**
    a. They had a car power shake.
    b. They are tireless. (Get it?)
    c. They are all fueled up.
    d. Of course they stop, silly; aren't you
       looking?

Buzz Lightyear Astro Blasters

Port of Entry
1. Who is welcome?
    a. Space Cadets
    b. Space Rangers
    c. Toys
    d. Visitors from the planet "Z"

2. "Red Alert" Why?
    a. Buzz Lightyear has gone missing.
    b. Planet "Z" is going to collide with earth!
    c. Little Green Men have taken control of the
       Space Cruisers.
    d. Star Command is under attack.

3. Find the XP Space Cruiser operating
instructions. What is number two on the
diagram?
    a. The blasters   b. The headlight
    c. The engine   d. The joystick

4. What does Buzz want most of us to
concentrate on?
    a. Those Green Men
    b. Galactic Enemy No. 1
    c. Those robots
    d. Anything that moves, Space Ranger.

Main Waiting Area

5. What is being used as Buzz's big screen?
    a. A hand-held video game
    b. A chalkboard
    c. An Etch A Sketch
    d. A computer monitor

6. Who is wanted?
    a. Evil Emperor Zurg
    b. All invaders from the planet "Z"
    c. Galactic Enemy No. 1
    d. All of the above
    e. Only 'a' and 'b'

7. What will your targets be, Space Cadets?
    a. Everything with a "Z"
    b. All the green invaders
    c. Anything that looks evil
    d. "X" marks the spot

8. What can be found in sector 7?
    a. A square planet
    b. A planet with rings around it
    c. Batteries floating in space
    d. Robotic space crabs

9. Who is peeking at you through the window in the door?
    a. Buzz Lightyear   b. Emperor Zurg
    c. Mickey Mouse   d. A three-eyed green
                               guy

10. Locate the number 020464. Where can it be found?
    a. It's the part number for the batteries preferred at Space Command.
    b. On the coordinates for sector C
    c. On Buzz Lightyear's badge
    d. On the score-keeping screen for a Little Green Man

Launch Area

11. Treasure Hunt Time! Look at the mural behind the ride vehicles. See if you can find the following for 1 point each.

- ☐ A robotic dog
- ☐ Someone losing their head
- ☐ Someone flying out of the back of their ship
- ☐ The word "Pow"
- ☐ A robot with a propeller on its head
- ☐ A flag with a "Z" on it
- ☐ Three red rings
- ☐ Yellow teeth
- ☐ Someone with wings
- ☐ A spring

12. What do the Little Green Men stand on?
   a. Batteries
   b. Each other
   c. Computer parts
   d. A large walkie-talkie

13. Find the number 112164. Where is it located?
   a. On a computer screen operated by the Green Squadron
   b. On the operating instructions for the Astro Blasters
   c. On the targeting instructions
   d. On the coordinates of sector 8

14. Find a Little Green Man with two eyes shut and one open. What is he doing?
   a. Winking at you   b. Aiming
   c. Sleeping with one eye open
   d. Trying to read something that is too high up for him

15. What is Star Command's symbol?
    a. A planet with a ring and spots
    b. A star and a rocket with fire coming out the back
    c. A planet with a ring, a rocket, and wings
    d. A flag with a sun and two stars on it

16. According to the Planets of the Galactic Alliance Chart, to what sector will your secret mission take you?
    a. Sector 8 to planet "K'afooel'ch"
    b. Sector 7 to planet "blue planet"
    c. Sector 6 to planet "poprock"
    d. Sector 9 to planet "Z"

17. Check the Planets of the Galactic Alliance Chart again. Which of the following planets is not on that chart?
    a. Greegooll-Zbokk   b. Green planet
    c. K'afooel'ch   d. Bridolnz
    e. Hey, wait a minute; those are all on the chart!
    f. Are you kidding me, Star Command. None of those places is charted in known space!

Disneyland Monorail

1. Treasure Hunt Time! Soon you will be whisked away to Downtown Disney on the Monorail. While you wait for your speedy transport see how many of these treasures you can unearth.

- ❏ Mariner
- ❏ Barnacles
- ❏ Four life preservers
- ❏ Seafarer
- ❏ Three waterfalls
- ❏ A conch shell
- ❏ A glass Monorail train
- ❏ Explorer
- ❏ A three-dimensional sun
- ❏ A starfish
- ❏ Neptune
- ❏ An arrow
- ❏ Argonaut
- ❏ Three blue-and-white checked flags
- ❏ A stalactite
- ❏ A wave
- ❏ The number 5

2. Extra points!!! For 3 bonus points, what year was the Monorail introduced into Disneyland?

a. 1948   b. 1959
c. 2005   d. 1978

3. Collection Time! If you are still waiting to board, this is a great time to work on your Collections. See page 13 if you're short of ideas.

Disneyland Railroad Station

1. Treasure Hunt Time! Try to find the following treasures before boarding time.

- ❏ A motor oil shake
- ❏ A blue car
- ❏ A pen
- ❏ A car that sparkles
- ❏ A bow tie
- ❏ A brown car
- ❏ A question mark
- ❏ A green car
- ❏ A reason to be "thankful"
- ❏ An orange car
- ❏ Fries you would never want to eat
- ❏ A yellow car
- ❏ A single white glove
- ❏ A manhole
- ❏ The Matterhorn
- ❏ A blue-and-white pennant
- ❏ A picture of a wheelchair and an arrow
- ❏ A yellow triangle with a flashing light at its tip

2. Collection Time! If you are still waiting to board your train, this is a great time to work on Collections.

Finding Nemo Submarine Voyage

1. Listen closely. Someone is being very greedy and yelling "mine, mine, mine." Who is it?
   a. A little girl holding Nemo in a bag
   b. The seagulls on the buoy
   c. Bruce, the big shark
   d. A kid trying to grab his sister's ice cream cone

2. There are often food venders in this area. Look around for them and give yourself 1 point for each different food vender you spot. Add a bonus point if you can find a healthy snack for sale.

3. The submarines all have numbers on them. Collect the numbers 0 through 9 by crossing off each number as you find it. Count each digit separately when you see a number with more than one. For example, if you saw 37, you'd cross off 3 and 7.

   0 1 2 3 4 5 6 7 8 9

The Finding Nemo ride first opened at Disneyland in 2007.

4. Is this ride older or younger than you?
   Older / Younger

5. Is it older or younger than Dad?
   Older / Younger

6. Is there anyone in your family younger than this ride?

   Yes / No

7. Treasure Hunt Time! Try to find these items before your submarine descends into the deep.

   - [ ] A Monorail train
   - [ ] Sounds of the Sasquatch from the Matterhorn
   - [ ] A bell ringing
   - [ ] Autopia cars: try to spot red, blue, green, yellow, and brown (1 point for finding all five)
   - [ ] The sound of a waterfall
   - [ ] A door with red and green lights above it
   - [ ] The Marine Observation Outpost
   - [ ] TL95
   - [ ] A life preserver
   - [ ] The saltwater supply
   - [ ] The word "caution"
   - [ ] Three seagulls
   - [ ] A real live bird
   - [ ] Someone doing an impression of a *Finding Nemo* character

8. Collection Time! If you are still waiting to submerge, why not work on a Collection?

Innoventions

1. Treasure Hunt Time! While you wait to enter Innoventions, keep your eyes on the building as it turns slowly around. Look closely at the mural on the building and see how many of the treasures in the list below you can locate in the mural before you go inside. Each item is worth 1 point.

- ❏ A red hot-air balloon
- ❏ A bicyclist
- ❏ A robot chef
- ❏ A spaceship shaped like a V
- ❏ A cruise ship
- ❏ A surfer
- ❏ A robot waving
- ❏ A solid gold branch with gold leaves
- ❏ A man with too many arms and legs
- ❏ The word Disneyland
- ❏ A gold man writing with a pencil
- ❏ A windsurfer
- ❏ A monorail system (in the mural)
- ❏ A camera
- ❏ A robotic dog being taken for a stroll on a leash
- ❏ A robot wearing a red bow tie
- ❏ A robotic kitty cat crouching
- ❏ A gold person pouring more gold
- ❏ A couple waving through the front window of their vehicle
- ❏ The letters 'a,' 'b,' and 'c' (1 point for finding all three)
- ❏ An old-style rocket ship (in the mural)
- ❏ An umbrella handle sticking out of a large vase

- ❑ Three men working on an assembly line
- ❑ A TV screen with Mickey Mouse ears on it
- ❑ A woman reading a book
- ❑ Two men wearing hard hats

2. Extra points!!! For 5 bonus points, find the clock that is hidden somewhere on the Innoventions building.

Space Mountain

Outside Queue

1. As you enter the ride you will see a sign describing Space Mountain. According to the sign which of the following is true? **FP**

    a. Space Mountain takes place in the dark.
    b. You must be at least 11 years old to go on Space Mountain.
    c. Space Mountain has sudden stops.
    d. Space Mountain turns upside down.
    e. Both 'a' and 'c'
    f. All of the above

2. Space Mountain is bordered on one side by a space-age restaurant. What is the name of the restaurant? **FP**

    a. Subs in Space   b. Sterns Sundays
    c. Pizza Port   d. Galactic Cantina

3. What is being provided to a thirsty galaxy?
    a. Milkshakes   b. Refreshment
    c. Drinks   d. Space sodas

4. What is providing a mist shower to people down below?
   a. A giant soda bottle
   b. A fountain
   c. A rocket ship
   d. A gardener with a hose

5. What has been made into a rocket that does not normally blast off into outer space?
   a. A cola bottle   b. A hamburger
   c. An elephant   d. A car

6. What is the rocket ship's name?
   a. Galaxy 1   b. Moonliner
   c. Star Racer   d. The Achiever

7. Where could you go to play video games?
   a. The Black Hole
   b. Astro Gamer
   c. Galactic Fun Center
   d. Starcade

Outside-Inside Treasure Hunt
8. Treasure Hunt Time! See if you can find these out-of-this-world treasures.
   - ❑ A life-size X-wing
   - ❑ A helipad
   - ❑ A collection of satellite dishes
   - ❑ A picture of Saturn (Tip: It's small. Look toward the restaurant from outside.)
   - ❑ At least five pictures of robots
   - ❑ Space age umbrellas
   - ❑ Something striped in red and white
   - ❑ A gold arrow
   - ❑ The spirit of refreshment
   - ❑ An all blue planet
   - ❑ A long narrow window through which you can see the very top of a rocket ship.

Inside Queue

9. Listen carefully. What should all personnel do? **FP**
   a. Prepare for blastoff.
   b. Fasten all safety restraints.
   c. Put on space gear.
   d. Clear the launch platform.

10. What does "Roger" mean? **FP**
    a. Yes, I understand.
    b. No, I don't understand.
    c. Say that again.
    d. I don't know, but they sure say it a lot. Maybe it's the captain's name.

11. What is numbered 77? **FP**
    a. Your flight
    b. The space station
    c. The giant spaceship
    d. There are 77 personnel at this port.

The Big Ship

12. When you reach the large spaceship, look it over. How many thrusters does it have? **FP**
    a. 2   b. 3
    c. 4   d. 5

13. How many portholes look into the main chamber of the spaceship? **FP**
    a. 6   b. 8
    c. 10   d. 12

14. Can you find SMS-077? **FP**
    Yes / No

15. Can you find a container holding water? **FP**
    Yes / No

16. Can you locate DL 05? **FP**
    Yes / No

17. Collection Time! Still waiting to soar into space? Work on a Collection or two.

Star Tours—
The Adventures Continue

Outside Queue
A long time ago in a queue not so far away there was a bit of a wait to enter the spaceport. If you will be waiting outside for a time, the next few questions are for you. If not, move ahead to the next section.

1. If you look around, you may find a picture of the StarSpeeder you will ride on today. How many doors does it have?
    a. 4   b. 5
    c. 6   d. 7

2. In the space mural outside, there is a spacecraft that looks a lot like something else here at Disneyland. What does it resemble?
    a. A ship that looks like the Monorail
    b. A ship that is flown by the three-eyed Little Green Men
    c. A ship that looks like Mickey Mouse's head
    d. A ship that looks like Space Mountain

3. What is the name of the intergalactic souvenir shop nearby?
    a. Jedi Junction
    b. Storeport
    c. Little Green Men Store Command
    d. Galactic Goodies

4. What is 1401?
   a. R2-D2's ship
   b. The number of this spaceport
   c. The number of the Red R2-D2 unit's ship
   d. I think it might just be the number of
      people in this line.

5. Treasure Hunt Time! See how many of these spacey treasures you can find before you blast off.

- ❏ A porthole peeper
- ❏ R2-D2
- ❏ A red R2-D2-like droid
- ❏ A green R2-D2-like droid
- ❏ A spacecraft with red-and-white stripes on it
- ❏ Four planets with rings
- ❏ A cratered planet
- ❏ The Death Star (a spaceship that is round with a single crater on it)
- ❏ A flying saucer
- ❏ Astronaut Mickey
- ❏ A high peak
- ❏ A golden sphere
- ❏ A planet with wings
- ❏ A robot

Extra Queue Room
If the line is particularly long, you will go through an extra queue room. It is oval shaped and has a space mural on the walls. If you enter it, play this game. If not, skip ahead to the next section.

6. Oval Queue Room Game
In *Star Wars*, the good guys are the Jedi and the bad guys are the Sith. They represent the light and dark sides of the Force. Perhaps they are hiding among you. To play, you must choose the light or dark side (if multiple people are playing,

split into a light team and a dark team). Now look among your fellow passengers for blue and red clothing. The Jedi will be wearing blue and the Sith, red. People who are wearing both colors are conflicted and the first player (or team) to spot them, wins their allegiance.

The battle between the dark and the light will be decided by which side gets the most members. To make it more fun, instead of just counting the number of people in the queue room who are wearing each color, you must find people wearing your color who also fit the descriptions below. Each description can be counted only once—by one side or the other. For example, if the light side finds a person with a hat who is also wearing blue, "A person wearing a hat" goes to the light side. Sorry, light side, but blue jeans do not count.

A person wearing a hat
  ❑ Dark side   ❑ Light side
A person with a purse
  ❑ Dark side   ❑ Light side
A person with a backpack
  ❑ Dark side   ❑ Light side
A person carrying a bag from a gift shop
  ❑ Dark side   ❑ Light side
A person carrying a stuffed animal
  ❑ Dark side   ❑ Light side
A person wearing Mickey Mouse ears
  ❑ Dark side   ❑ Light side
A person wearing a Disney character
  ❑ Dark side   ❑ Light side
A person with a single ponytail
  ❑ Dark side   ❑ Light side
A person with two ponytails
  ❑ Dark side   ❑ Light side
A person with braids
  ❑ Dark side   ❑ Light side

A person carrying a child
    ❏ Dark side   ❏ Light side

A person eating something
    ❏ Dark side   ❏ Light side

A person drinking something
    ❏ Dark side   ❏ Light side

A person in a dress or a skirt
    ❏ Dark side   ❏ Light side

A person with a jacket
    ❏ Dark side   ❏ Light side

A person wearing stripes
    ❏ Dark side   ❏ Light side

A person with a beard
    ❏ Dark side   ❏ Light side

People holding hands
    ❏ Dark side   ❏ Light side

In The Spaceport *FP*

You are now entering the spaceport. In this area you will have to listen and look for answers. You may not be able to answer all the questions in the time you are in the area. That is OK because it means you are getting closer to the ride!

Note: Questions coming from the screen or the robots will come in no particular order, so you may want to check ahead a bit. (If you don't have time to answer the questions now, you can always see what you remember when you're taking a break or waiting in another line.)

7. As you enter the spaceport, you will pass a door you're not allowed to enter. What lies beyond the door? *FP*

    a. A special lounge for frequent space travelers

    b. A droid lounge

    c. Docking bay 94

    d. A restricted customs area

8. What is the current security threat level? **FP**
   - a. 5
   - b. Red
   - c. 2
   - d. Orange

9. What is R2-D2 fixing? **FP**
   - a. The power couplings
   - b. The hyperdrive
   - c. The thrusters
   - d. Absolutely nothing—that lazy, overgrown scrap pile!

10. What is every StarSpeeder equipped with? **FP**
   - a. A free checked-baggage area
   - b. The most reliable pilot
   - c. The most legroom
   - d. The widest seats
   - e. All of the above
   - f. All but 'a'

11. On what planet can you visit the planet's core? **FP**
   - a. Coruscant
   - b. Tatooine
   - c. Naboo
   - d. Pluto

12. What is the weather forecast for Cloud City? **FP**
   - a. Snowy
   - b. Sunny and bright
   - c. Dust storms in the afternoon
   - d. Cloudy, of course

13. Who does C-3PO think is an ungrateful little twit? **FP**
   - a. A passenger who did not bother to say thank you
   - b. All scanning droids—and they're not very bright either
   - c. R2-D2
   - d. The head droid at the spaceport. ("He thinks he does everything.")

14. What must all interplanetary travelers present? **FP**
   a. Visas   b. Photo ID
   c. Current passport   d. All of the above
   e. Only 'a' and 'c'

15. What does a Tatooine vacation have? **FP**
   a. Everything under the suns
   b. Really rocking dust twisters
   c. Tattoos
   d. Some of the biggest slugs this side of
      Endor

16. What is the flight number to Coruscant? **FP**
   a. 492   b. 705
   c. 814   d. 1025

17. Who should you try to catch a glimpse of when visiting Naboo? **FP**
   a. Jar Jar Binks   b. The Queen
   c. The Emperor   d. Elvis

18. What planet does C-3PO think is most beautiful? **FP**
   a. Endor   b. Tatooine
   c. Hoth   d. Naboo

19. Something keeps happening to R2-D2 while he works. What is it? **FP**
   a. He gets hit with steam.
   b. He is forced to listen to C-3PO complain.
   c. He is spun around.
   d. He is zapped with electricity.
   e. All of the above
   f. Only 'a' and 'b'

20. Where can you party all night long? **FP**
   a. In Tatooine at the Cantina
   b. On Coruscant in the famous club district
   c. On Endor in the forest party shack

d. In a StarSpeeder 2000. They are equipped with a party room and custom disco balls.

21. Can you find a mini image of R2-D2? **FP**
Yes / No

22. Can you find an alien creature with a fish head? **FP**
Yes / No

23. Which of these locations isn't listed in the spaceport directory? **FP**
    a. Lightspeeder Lounge
    b. Customs
    c. Security
    d. Observation Deck
    e. They are all listed.

24. What is required for all droid passengers? **FP**
    a. Proof of ownership
    b. A restraining bolt
    c. A cargo payment receipt
    d. Nothing, droids are not allowed as passengers.

Baggage Scan Area **FP**

25. Hey, that baggage droid looks like he could use a little of your help. Here is a list of things commonly found in the scanned luggage of interplanetary travelers. Perhaps if you are good enough at spotting them, you will find an awesome job here scanning luggage.

☐ A stuffed animal that the droid thinks is alive

☐ A stormtrooper helmet

☐ A Buzz Lightyear doll—to infinity and beyond

☐ A group of droid heads that like to say "Roger"

- ❏ A Mickey Mouse hat
- ❏ A sorcerer's hat
- ❏ A genie's lamp
- ❏ A stowaway
- ❏ Boxer shorts with a heart pattern
- ❏ A droid lying on its back and having a look around
- ❏ A football
- ❏ Guns
- ❏ A lightsaber
- ❏ Extra hands
- ❏ A little ball shooting light
- ❏ WALL-E (a square robot with tank wheels and binocular eyes)
- ❏ A coil of rope
- ❏ A camera
- ❏ Glasses
- ❏ Flip flops
- ❏ A head in a crystal ball
- ❏ Bagpipes
- ❏ A superhero costume
- ❏ Goofy's hat
- ❏ Tennis shoes
- ❏ A droid in pieces
- ❏ A monkey playing the drums
- ❏ A computer
- ❏ A bag belonging to Lando Calrissian
- ❏ Goggles
- ❏ A C-3PO head
- ❏ A baseball hat

Silhouette Area *FP*

26. See how many of these silhouettes you can find before you space out.

- ❏ C-3PO
- ❏ A person carrying a purse
- ❏ A stormtrooper
- ❏ Something that gets shot down
- ❏ R2-D2

- ❑ Someone with a touch pad recording information
- ❑ R2-D2 getting pushed around
- ❑ Two people bowing in greeting
- ❑ A camera pestering a passenger
- ❑ A Jawa (a short person in a hooded robe)
- ❑ People holding hands
- ❑ A person stretching from the top of the window all the way to the bottom
- ❑ R2-D2 doing a Mickey Mouse impression
- ❑ Someone dropping something
- ❑ Watto (A pudgy flying passenger)
- ❑ Someone carrying a stack of boxes
- ❑ A family of Ewoks (fuzzy teddy bear-like creatures)
- ❑ Someone putting up his hood
- ❑ A Jedi using a mind trick
- ❑ Jar Jar Binks getting a ride (a tall creature with buggy eyes and long floppy ears)

Body scan area *FP*

? **Pop Quiz!** Soon it will be time for your full body scan, which is required of all interplanetary passengers, no exceptions. Listen carefully to the body-scan droid while you are in his area. Then see how many of these questions you can answer from memory.

27. What is the body-scan droid's favorite thing to say? *FP*

a. "Nothing to see here."

b. "Keep it moving."

c. "Respect the droids."

d. "Is that a Wookie or is it your boyfriend?"

28. What is the body-scan droid not programmed to deal with? **FP**
   a. Young humans
   b. Rabid Gungans
   c. Your personal problems
   d. Begging

29. What is a job in security? **FP**
   a. "A job in security"
   b. "My lot in life"
   c. "A great place to throw my weight around"
   d. "The most important thing any droid will ever do"

30. According to the body-scan droid, why are no liquids allowed onboard the flight? **FP**
   a. "Because I said so, that is all the reason you need, human."
   b. "The shuttle was built by droids who did not think to put in a bathroom."
   c. "Humans are known to be the clumsiest life form in the galaxy. Enough said."
   d. "Because it is rule number 458.2 in the Passenger's Conduct Handbook provided to you at booking."

31. The body-scan droid is very concerned with how the line is moving. According to him, when is it OK to stop moving? **FP**
   a. When frozen in carbonite
   b. When he says "Stop, Humans!"
   c. When you have boarded your spacecraft and are belted into your seat
   d. When you bump into the person in front of you

32. How does the body-scan droid "like it"? **FP**
   a. He likes it when everything is moving smoothly.
   b. He likes it when all of the humans have

boarded their flights and he can power
down.
c. He likes it with cream and sugar.
d. He does not like it; what's to like?

33. The body-scan droid remarks on someone's
strength. What does he say about it? *FP*
    a. "Do you need some help with your bag
       mister? The kid next to you looks strong."
    b. "You look strong enough to deadlift Jabba
       the Hut."
    c. "You look strong enough to pull the ears
       off a Gondar."
    d. "Wow, that guy looks strong, must be part
       Wookie."

34. What advice does the body-scan droid give
you for your tour? *FP*
    a. "Don't hire Gungans as tour guides or
       bodyguards."
    b. "Don't do anything I wouldn't do, and I
       wouldn't do anything."
    c. "Stay out of imperial sectors."
    d. "If you play games with the natives, let the
       Wookie win!"

35. Why could the body-scan droid use a little
help? *FP*
    a. He is trying to practice Jedi mind tricks
       from his Jedi-by-mail course. He needs
       a passenger with a very weak mind to
       practice on.
    b. He is about to power off and needs
       someone to continue the scanning process.
    c. He is running behind on his quota of
       passengers detained and would like
       volunteers.
    d. He accidentally wiped his memory and
       can't remember who he is.

36. What note was left for the driver of a brown landspeeder Model X-34? **FP**

    a. "This area is for the loading and unloading of droids only."

    b. "Parked in my space, you are. Have you towed, I will."

    c. "I find your lack of parking skill disturbing."

    d. "Chewie tells me you are looking for passage to the Alderaan system."

37. Some woman tried to waltz past security with something she wasn't allowed to have. What was it? **FP**

    a. Two cinnamon buns in her hair

    b. She had a small Ewok in her purse.

    c. She concealed a pod-racing betting form in her book.

    d. She had the plans for a Death Star stashed inside her droid.

38. How would the body-scan droid like you to act? **FP**

    a. More like a droid

    b. Like a more intelligent life form

    c. Like you are paying attention

    d. Less suspicious

39. What is the most fun thing he can think of? **FP**

    a. Scanning you

    b. A relaxing oil bath

    c. Assisting you with anything you might need

    d. He is not programmed to think of anything fun.

40. What is this job to a security droid? **FP**

    a. His primary program

    b. An opportunity to be bored out of his mind

c. Just a job
d. "It's awful. Brain the size of a planet and I'm doing this."

41. What language is the body-scan droid shocked that you do not speak? **FP**
   a. Wookineaase   b. Ewakein
   c. Binary   d. Bochi

42. What does he commend a gentleman for doing a good job of? **FP**
   a. Bumping into the person in front of him before stopping
   b. Making his mind a complete blank
   c. Standing upright
   d. Nothing

43. Why isn't he thanking you for your cooperation? **FP**
   a. "I am not programmed to be thankful."
   b. "I am not a mealy-mouthed protocol droid."
   c. "It is my job to be as intimidating as possible."
   d. "Since your cooperation is mandatory, no thanks seem necessary."

44. There are no overhead compartments in the StarSpeeder, true or false? **FP**

45. What does the body-scan droid say to those traveling with small children? **FP**
   a. "Good Luck"
   b. "There is absolutely no riding on a parent's lap or what have you."
   c. "Children with more than two arms must be properly restrained."
   d. "I am sorry, but restraining bolts are for droid use only."

46. What does he feel is suspicious human behavior? **FP**
    a. Laughing   b. Sweating
    c. Blinking   d. Breathing
    e. All of the above   f. All but 'd'

47. What new program is he trying out? **FP**
    a. Human behavior simulator
    b. Speed scanning
    c. Small talk
    d. "American Idol"

48. What does the body-scan droid mistake someone's children for? **FP**
    a. Wookies   b. Jawas
    c. Master Yoda   d. Droids

49. How many different species of life forms can the scanner recognize? **FP**
    a. 6,000
    b. 10,000
    c. 14,000
    d. All known life forms

50. Is this the correct line for alien species? **FP**
    Yes / No

51. According to the body-scan droid, which is one of those funny words that just puts a smile on your face? **FP**
    a. Churro
    b. Supercalifragilisticexpialidocious
    c. Phlegm
    d. Diphthong

52. What restaurant does the scanning droid recommend? **FP**
    a. Mos Eisley Cantina
    b. Dexter's Diner

c. The restaurant at the end of the universe
d. The Spaceport Skyroom
e. He doesn't recommend human food. It smells just awful.

53. When the body-scan droid gets his wires wet, what happens? **FP**
  a. He gets the urge to put on his scuba gear and go for a swim.
  b. He shuts down, but it makes for a nice nap.
  c. He has to dry himself out with a hair dryer, which is a bit humiliating.
  d. He ends up repeating himself every 20 minutes.

54. What does he say to someone who looks familiar? **FP**
  a. "You look familiar, but then all humans look the same to me."
  b. "Hey, are you my long lost brother? No? What about sister?"
  c. "You look familiar; do you normally wear a large black helmet?"
  d. "Haven't I scanned you somewhere before?"

55. What must all passengers have? **FP**
  a. Tickets
  b. Flight glasses
  c. A pulse
  d. The ability to sit; "This means you, sir."

56. How long do the security droid's relationships last? **FP**
  a. 1 second
  b. 5 seconds
  c. 10 seconds
  d. Forever, he never forgets a face.

Tomorrowland Answers

Astro Orbitor
1) c. 12
2) Yes
3) b. Water
4) d. Toy Story 2
5) a. Pull the controller back toward yourself.
6) a. Push the controller away from yourself.
7-9) The answers depend on your family.
10) Number of items collected _____

Autopia
1) b. 55 smiles per hour
2) a. Chevron
3) d. Winner's Circle
4) Yes
5) b. 54 inches
6) c. Blue and white
7) a. Hit the car in front of you
8) b. Dusty
9) c. Motor oil
10) a. Your cares
11) d. Accelerate the
12) Total Letters found _____
13) Total Numbers found _____
14) a. 6.5 mph
15) b. They are tireless.

Buzz Lightyear Astro Blasters
Port of Entry
1) b. Space Rangers
2) d. Star Command is under attack.
3) a. The blasters
4) c. Those robots
Main Waiting Area
5) c. An Etch A Sketch
6) d. All of the above
7) a. Everything with a "Z"

8) b. A planet with rings around it

9) d. A three-eyed green guy

10) d. On the score-keeping screen for a Little Green Man

Launch Area

11) Total Treasures found _____

12) a. Batteries

13) b. On the operating instructions for the Astro Blasters

14) b. Aiming

15) c. A planet with a ring, a rocket, and wings

16) d. Sector 9 to planet "Z"

17) e. Hey, wait a minute; those are all on the chart!

Disneyland Monorail

1) Total Treasures found _____

2) b) 1959 (Collect 3 bonus points if you got this.)

3) Number of items collected _____

Disneyland Railroad: Tomorrowland Station

1) Total Treasures found _____

2) Number of items collected _____

Finding Nemo Submarine Voyage

1) b. The seagulls on the buoy

2) Number of different food venders spotted _____
   Add 1 bonus point if you spotted a healthy snack for sale.

3) Give yourself 1 point if you collected all 10 numbers.

4-6) These answers depend on your family.

7) Total Treasures found _____

8) Number of items collected _____

Innoventions

1) Total Treasures found _____

2) Add 5 bonus points if you spotted the clock. (Tip: It's in the sign for the Innoventions building.)

Space Mountain

1) e. Both 'a' and 'c'

2) c. Pizza Port

3) b. Refreshment

Space Mountain, cont'd.
4) c. A rocket ship
5) a. A cola bottle
6) b. Moonliner
7) d. Starcade

Outside-Inside Treasure Hunt
8) Total Treasures found _____

Inside Queue
9) d. Clear the launch platform
10) a. Yes, I understand.
11) b. The space station

The Big Ship
12) c. 4
13) c. 10
14) Yes
15) Yes. Remember, water is H_2O.
16) Yes
17) Number of items collected _____

Star Tours—The Adventures Continue
1) b. 5
2) d. A ship that looks like Space Mountain
3) c. Little Green Men Store Command
4) a. R2-D2's ship
5) Total Outdoor Treasures found _____

Extra Queue Room:
6) Oval Queue Room Game
Total Light Side points _____
Total Dark Side points _____

In The Spaceport
7) d. A restricted customs area
8) a. 5
9) b. The hyperdrive
10) f. All but 'a'
11) c. Naboo
12) d. Cloudy
13) c. R2-D2
14) e. Only 'a' and 'c'
15) a. Everything under the suns
16) c. 814
17) b. The Queen

18) d. Naboo

19) f. Only 'a' and 'b'

20) b. On Coruscant in the famous club district

21) Yes

22) Yes

23) b. Customs

24) a. Proof of ownership

Baggage Scan Area

25) Number of items found _____

1-2 items found: Don't quit your day job.

3-4 items found: Well, you probably won't be working here, but not bad for a human.

5-6 items found: I think there's a future here for you.

7 or more items found: You're hired. Please get fitted with a restraining bolt and get to work!

Silhouette Area

26) Total Silhouettes found _____

Body Scan Pop Quiz

27) b. "Keep it moving."

28) c. Your personal problems

29) a. "A job in security"

30) b. "The shuttle was built by droids who did not think to put in a bathroom."

31) d. When you bump into the person in front of you

32) a. He likes it when everything is moving smoothly.

33) c. "You look strong enough to pull the ears off a Gondar."

34) b. "Don't do anything I wouldn't do, and I wouldn't do anything."

35) d. He accidentally wiped his memory and can't remember who he is.

36) b. "Parked in my space, you are. Have you towed, I will."

37) a. Two cinnamon buns in her hair

38) d. Less suspicious

39) a. Scanning you

40) c. Just a job

41) c. Binary

42) b. Making his mind a complete blank

43) d. "Since your cooperation is mandatory, no thanks seem necessary."

Star Tours, cont'd.

44) True

45) a. "Good Luck"

46) e. All of the above

47) c. Small talk

48) b. Jawas

49) c. 14,000

50) No

51) a. Churro

52) b. Dexter's Diner

53) d. He ends up repeating himself every 20 minutes.

54) d. "Haven't I scanned you somewhere before?"

55) b. Flight glasses

56) b. 5 seconds

Frontierland

———◆———

Big Thunder Mountain Railroad

1. It's time to play **Mother Lode**.

You just ambled up to one of the best mines in these here parts. I reckin' you are welcome here at the Big Thunder Mine. That is unless you are a filthy claim-jumping varmint. It seems some snake is trying to put a spoke through the wheels of Big Thunder Mining Company by stealin' its gold! In fact, some dreadful big nuggets have gone missin' just since you rode into town, pardner.

Hear that! There may be a gold thief in yer group!

Here is how to play "Mother Lode":
Yer group picks one person to be the gold poacher. Everyone else plays sheriff. Yer gold poacher selects a spot within view as the hiding place for the stolen gold. (*Tip:* The queue offers many great hidey holes, but be sure to choose a place that will remain visible as you move along in the queue or the game won't work. If at any point the hiding place is no longer visible, the

poacher should pick a new hiding place and tell the sheriffs that the gold has been moved.)

It is the sheriffs' job to puzzle out where the poacher hid the gold. Taking turns, each sheriff asks a yes or no question about the hiding place. For example, "Is it hidden someplace on the ground?"

The sheriffs keep taking turns asking questions until someone thinks they've reckoned out where the gold is stashed and says, "The jig is up." If the sheriff's guess is correct, that player gets 5 points. If the sheriff is wrong, the poacher takes the points and re-hides the gold.

When the stash is found, the finder becomes the next poacher and the game starts over.

2. Jail Break

The sheriff has just reported that the county jail has lost track of a yellow-belly train-robbing outlaw by the name of Billy the Whistler. The Whistler is notorious for his love of trains, or as he likes to call them "choo choos." Before he robs a likely looking "choo choo" of the goods it is transporting, he always takes it for a very fast joy ride. As the trains in these here parts are always slower than molasses in January and have the finest safety records in the West, it is important to catch this lawbreaker and put him on the fast track back to the pokey.

The sheriff reckons the Whistler may be lurking in and around the local railroad tracks, particularly the tracks near gold mines. As there is a mine in yer area, the sheriff would be much obliged if you would keep an eye open and yer handcuffs handy, pardner.

To play the game, one of you must be the game keeper. That person will select "the Whistler" from within the suspicious-looking crowd cooling its heels in line with you. (The

Whistler is skilled at disguise. He could be hidin' as a man, a woman or a child.) Everyone else in yer group must take turns asking questions to narrow down the possibilities. For example, "Is the Whistler wearing a hat?" As soon as someone thinks they have discovered the Whistler, they must whisper their guess to the game keeper. Please avoid pointing though. Even train-obsessed, filthy outlaws hate to be pointed at.

Tip: This game can be played as many times as you like.

3. If you tire of huntin' down the lawless, this would be a good time to ponder on yer Collections. People wearing Disney pins and people texting would be good bets here.

Mark Twain Riverboat / Sailing Ship Columbia Loading Dock

1. What game is available while you wait?
    a. Darts   b. Chess
    c. Horseshoes   d. Pachinko

2. What is not allowed inside the waiting area?
    a. Cameras   b. Food and drink
    c. Balloons   d. Strollers

3. What color is the fire hydrant?
    a. Red   b. Yellow
    c. Orange   d. Red, white, and blue

4. Where is the big crate on the dock from?
    a. Wyoming   b. Louisiana
    c. Kansas   d. Mississippi

5. When was Becket & Paige Mercantile established?
    a. 1789   b. 1883
    c. 1903   d. 2000

6. A mining company's name is somewhere around you. What is the name?
    a. Olson Mines
    b. Mickey Mouse Mining
    c. Stratton Mining Co.
    d. Columbia Mining Association

7. What are the accomplishments of Mark Twain?
    a. Author, teacher, and chili-making champ
    b. Author, politician, and painter of picket fences
    c. Author, humorist, and occasional riverboat captain
    d. Author, horsemen, and man who could never tell a lie

8. Which is not a deck on the riverboat?
    a. Tom & Huck Deck
    b. Promenade Deck
    c. Texas Deck
    d. Pilot House

9. What is the claim to fame of the "Columbia Rediviva"?
    a. It was the fastest ship of its time.
    b. It was unsinkable.
    c. It was able to run on solar energy.
    d. It was the first American ship to circumnavigate the globe.

10. Which of the following is not a fact about the "Columbia Rediviva"?

    a. Its maximum crew was 30.

    b. It made its maiden voyage in 1786.

    c. It had 10 cannons.

    d. It was used to trade with China.

Pirate's Lair on Tom Sawyer Island

1. How many lanterns can you count in the raft waiting area?

    a. 3   b. 5

    c. 7   d. 9

2. Can you find two skulls and crossed swords?
    Yes / No

3. Someone is storing his sword in an unusual place. Where?

    a. Hanging in the overhead ropes

    b. Stuck in the mass of the raft

    c. Stuck deep in a treasure chest

    d. Hidden up high in the branches of a tree

4. What animal part can you find on each attendant?

    a. A shark's tooth around their neck

    b. A bear claw hanging from an earring

    c. A snakeskin belt

    d. A feather in their hat

5. Who discovered the "real pirate chest"?
   a. Tom, Huck, and Joe
   b. Tom Sawyer
   c. Captain Jack Sparrow
   d. Mark Twain

6. Treasure Hunt Time! How many treasures can you find before you sail for the island?
   ❑ A U.S. flag
   ❑ A crow's-nest
   ❑ A waterfall
   ❑ A waterwheel
   ❑ Two boxes in the air
   ❑ A makeshift bag made out of light brown fabric
   ❑ A pulley
   ❑ A large piece of fish netting
   ❑ A wooden Pirate's Lair plank
   ❑ A lifesaver
   ❑ A small smokestack

Frontierland Answers

Big Thunder Mountain Railroad
1) *Mother Lode* points:
Player 1 _____ Player 2 _____ Player 3 _____
Player 4 _____
2) *Jail Break* points:
Player 1 _____ Player 2 _____ Player 3 _____
Player 4 _____
3) Number of items collected _____

Mark Twain Riverboat /
Sailing Ship Columbia loading dock
1) b. Chess
2) d. Strollers
3) a. Red
4) d. Mississippi
5) b. 1883
6) c. Stratton Mining Co.
7) c. Author, humorist, and occasional riverboat captain
8) a. Tom & Huck Deck
9) d. It was the first American ship to circumnavigate the globe.
10) b. It made its maiden voyage in 1786.

Pirate's Lair on Tom Sawyer Island
1) c. 7
2) Yes
3) c. Stuck deep in a treasure chest
4) d. A feather in their hat
5) a. Tom, Huck, and Joe
6) Total Treasures found _____

Adventureland

Enchanted Tiki Room

1. Who sponsors the Tiki Room?
   a. Dole   b. Bank of America
   c. Chevron   d. None of the above

2. What is the flavor of Hawaii?
   a. Mango   b. Guava
   c. Coconut   d. Pineapple

3. What type of hands do you need to select the best pineapple?
   a. Skilled   b. Trained
   c. Large   d. Dainty

4. What is pineapple?
   a. King of fruits
   b. A symbol of hospitality
   c. Both 'a' and 'b'

5. Who caused the people to change to his time?
   a. The king of Hawaii
   b. The sun god
   c. The top pineapple farmer

6. Who is balancing the earth?
   a. Rongo   b. Ngendei
   c. Koro   d. Maui

7. Who makes flowers sing and tikis smile?
    a. Koro   b. Pele
    c. Tangaroa-ru   d. Ngendei

8. Who flew the world's first kite?
    a. Rongo   b. Pele
    c. Tangaroa-ru   d. Koro

9. Who made the sun keep regular hours?
    a. Rongo   b. Ngendei
    c. Pele   d. Maui

10. Who has a clock on his face?
    a. Ngendei   b. Maui
    c. Tangaroa-ru   d. Pele

11. Who is the father of all gods and goddesses?
    a. Tangaroa   b. Rongo
    c. Ngendei   d. Maui

12. What do the door handles look like?
    a. Toucan heads   b. Hands
    c. Fish   d. Flowers

13. Who taught the women and men to dance?
    a. Tangaroa-ru   b. Pele
    c. Koro   d. Ngendei

14. Who blows their bloomin' top right off?
    a. Pele   b. Maui
    c. Tangaroa-ru   d. Rongo

15. From where does new life fall?
    a. From the arms of Rongo
    b. From the limbs of Tangaroa
    c. From the mouth of Maui
    d. From the heart of Tangaroa-ru

16. Who is such a hothead that fire comes out
    the top?
    a. Ngendei   b. Hina Kuluua
    c. Tangaroa-ru   d. Pele

17. Who often travel together?
   a. Maui and Rongo
   b. Hina Kuluua and Tangaroa-ru
   c. Tangaroa-ru and Tangaroa
   d. Koro and Ngendei

Indiana Jones Adventure

Outside Queue

1. As you enter the line, look at the sign. What does it say continues? **FP**
   a. The adventure   b. The story
   c. The hero   d. The legend

2. As you start along the line, you will see a makeshift campsite. It appears that someone had been enjoying refreshments. What do you see there?
   a. A tea kettle
   b. Several white cups
   c. Bones left over from dinner
   d. A camp cooking pot with lid
   e. All of the above
   f. All but 'c'

3. Can you find someone's clean pants hanging out to dry?
   Yes / No

4. Where is the number 11204 to be found?
   a. It's the address number on a crate.
   b. It's the license plate number of the Jeep.
   c. It's on an artifact identification tag.
   d. It is a map coordinate.

5. There is a building marked "Danger." Why?
   a. Scorpion infestation
   b. High voltage
   c. Guard dogs
   d. Loose rubble

6. What symbol appears on the door of the Jeep?
   a. A triangle containing an eye
   b. A skull and crossbones
   c. A snake
   d. A bullwhip

Temple View

7. You will soon see the temple in front of you. It appears to be crumbling. There are six columns. What is featured on the columns?
   a. Eyes   b. Deities
   c. Snakes   d. Elephants

8. On the ground, you can see the heads of statues that have crumbled. How many do you count? _____

9. As you are walking up to the temple entrance, can you find a crate that is moving? (Hint: Look all around you.)
   Yes / No

10. As you wait to enter the temple, listen to the sounds around you. What do you hear? *FP*
   a. Tarzan yelling, lions roaring, and monkeys shrieking
   b. Lions roaring, monkeys shrieking, and gorillas roaring
   c. Tarzan yelling, monkeys shrieking, and elephants trumpeting
   d. Elephants trumpeting, Tarzan yelling, and gorillas roaring
   e. Lions and tigers and bears! Oh my.

Inside The Temple

11. You will come to a painted image of a man wearing an eye around his neck and pouring something. What is he pouring? *FP*

    a. Water and treasure b. Wine and water
    c. Snakes and jewels   d. Mud and gold

12. Why did the entry to the temple avoid detection for so long? (This is a hard one!) *FP*

    a. It was buried in rubble.
    b. It was covered with foliage.
    c. It was behind a secret door.
    d. It was guarded by curses.

13. In a letter to Sallah, Indy comments on rotten luck. To what is he referring? (Another hard one!) *FP*

    a. The temple is infested with snakes.
    b. The temple is unstable and dangerous to explore.
    c. He has misplaced his fedora and feels unlucky without it.
    d. Reports of the temple have hit the news.

14. Can you find a cobra holding an unfortunate person? *FP*

    Yes / No

Booby Trap

15. You have entered an area known as the flooded maze. What should you be on the lookout for? *FP*

    a. Loose rubble
    b. Unexpected water bursts
    c. Quicksand
    d. Dart-throwing natives

16. Can you find an eye carved into the wall? *FP*

    Yes / No

17. Who or what should you not disturb? **FP**
   a. The bats
   b. The temple guardians
   c. The archaeologist at work
   d. The skeletons at rest

18. Did you encounter stalactites or stalagmites? (Hard one again.) **FP**
   a. Stalactites   b. Stalagmites
   c. Both   d. Neither

19. Why should you watch your head? **FP**
   a. Low ceilings   b. Hanging vines
   c. Sharp spikes   d. Bat droppings

20. You will come upon a number of large spikes that seem to have ended the expedition for some who came before you. How many full skeletons can you find? **FP**
   a. 5   b. 2
   c. 4   d. 3

21. What article of clothing can be found on the spikes? **FP**
   a. A shirt   b. A boot
   c. A handkerchief   d. A hat

22. What shape stones must you not step on? **FP**
   a. Diamond   b. Square
   c. Eye-shaped   d. Circle

Large Temple Room
23. Treasure Hunt Time! You have arrived at a large room with bamboo platforms and paintings on the high ceiling. See if you can collect the treasures below before leaving this chamber. **FP**
   ❏   An eye with vines growing out of it
   ❏   A forked tongue
   ❏   At least two pulleys

❑ A crate containing a vase
❑ A barrel
❑ A lit lantern
❑ Archaeological expedition brushes
❑ A red hook
❑ A stool
❑ At least two different types of ladders
❑ A red wheel
❑ Someone depicted walking with a snake cane
❑ Someone holding a basket of fruit
❑ An old radio
❑ A reason for caution

24. Locate a stone elephant. How many people are riding on the elephant? *FP*

a. 0
b. 1
c. 2
d. 3

Movie Room

? **Pop Quiz!** Watch the movie and then see how many of the following questions you can answer about what you've just seen.

25. What was the name of the temple you entered? *FP*

a. The Temple of the Forbidden Eye
b. The Temple of the Snake
c. The Temple of the Forbidden Snake
d. The Temple of the Eye of Destiny

26. If you peeked into the eyes of the idol, what was your next stop? *FP*

a. The grave
b. The end of the line
c. The gates of doom
d. There were no more stops for you.

27. What should you keep your "Eye On" now? **FP**

    a. The prize   b. The globe

    c. The ground   d. The road

28. Did you find a sign telling you to take heed? **FP**

    Yes / No

29. What might Indiana Jones solve? **FP**

    a. The riddle of the temple's eye

    b. The riddle of 1,000 snakes

    c. The riddle of steel

    d. The riddle of the lost tourists

30. What were the headlines of the newspaper shown during the movie? **FP**

    a. Incredible Discovery of Ancient Temple

    b. Temple Claims More Lives

    c. Man Visits Temple, Returns with Gold

    d. Tourists Lost in Temple

31. Host Sallah showed you a vehicle. Who or what was in the vehicle that shouldn't have been there? **FP**

    a. Indiana Jones

    b. A snake

    c. A skeleton

    d. A man removing Mickey Mouse ears

32. What did Indiana Jones claim that the chamber contained? **FP**

    a. An ancient tablet with important writings on it

    b. A fountain of snakes

    c. A chamber of destiny

    d. A solid gold eye

End of Pop Quiz

33. What were the greedy globetrotters ready for? **FP**
   a. A peek into the beyond
   b. A supernatural shopping spree
   c. A life of leisure
   d. Absolutely nothing; they should probably have called it a day.

34. What invention did your host Sallah refer to as excellent? **FP**
   a. The safety belts
   b. The car
   c. The GPS tracking device
   d. Indy's hat

35. What according to host Sallah would be dangerous, very dangerous indeed? **FP**
   a. Entering the temple
   b. Looking into the eyes of the idol
   c. Riding in the cars through the rough terrain
   d. Angering the snake god

36. What did the ancient idol lure visitors with? **FP**
   a. Visions of the future
   b. Eternal youth
   c. Earthly riches
   d. All of the above

37. The newscaster told us that Sallah recently visited the observatory of the future. What did he hope Sallah would now be able to tell us? **FP**
   a. How long our lives would be
   b. Where the next great treasure was to be discovered
   c. Who would win the World Series
   d. What the stock market would do next week

38. What were many tourists claiming about their visits to the Temple of the Forbidden Eye? **FP**
   a. That loved ones had disappeared inside
   b. That they found great knowledge and wealth
   c. That they saw nothing; the temple was a hoax
   d. That they had never felt quite right since setting foot in the place

Jungle Cruise

Queue Entry

1. Look at the decorations around the Jungle Cruise sign. Which of the following descriptions is incorrect?
   a. There are five spears sticking out of it.
   b. Each spear has dried grass hanging from it.
   c. There is a head with a beak on it.
   d. Tours depart daily.

2. What year was the Jungle Navigation Co. established?
   a. 1892   b. 1899
   c. 1911   d. 1946

3. From what dock do the riverboats depart?
   a. The great dock of London
   b. Adventureland Dock
   c. Schweitzer Dock
   d. Zanzibar Dock

4. Who or what should you not feed?
   a. Ducks
   b. Crocodiles
   c. Yourself
   d. Elephants (We don't want them coming too close and stepping on the boats!)

5. Treasure Hunt Time! If you look around you should be able to find many things that belong on or around boats. Here are some to find:

- ❏ Floats
- ❏ Fishing net
- ❏ Steering wheel
- ❏ Oars
- ❏ An oar with a bite in it
- ❏ Ship's bell
- ❏ Hook
- ❏ Propellers
- ❏ A blue tool box
- ❏ A plane for woodwork
- ❏ A gas can
- ❏ Shovels

6. What has a 2,500-mile guarantee?
   a. The Congo Queen
   b. The Jeep
   c. Aero Eastern Motor Oil
   d. Rongo the Elephant

7. There are three pieces of framed art on the wall that feature animals you might find in the jungle. Which of the following is not pictured in any of them?
   a. Elephant   b. Butterfly
   c. Hyena   d. Tiger

Booking Office
8. Treasure Hunt Time! Look around the booking office area. Can you find the items listed below?
- ❏ A seal press
- ❏ A fan
- ❏ Two safari booking ledgers
- ❏ A receipt stacker with a large pin sticking out
- ❏ *National Geographic* magazine

9. Who or what is "Wagons-Lits.Cook"?
   a. A travel agent
   b. A boat captain
   c. A plane pilot
   d. A cargo chief

10. What should you ask about?
    a. The wildlife
    b. Food served on safari
    c. Our excellent service history
    d. Our package tours

11. What is the Jungle Queen?
    a. A boat
    b. The cruise office's pet cat
    c. The ruler of the Congo
    d. An elephant that the boat crew is
       particularly fond of

12. Treasure Hunt Time! Look around the booking, staging, and luggage areas of the Jungle Cruise office as you pass through. Can you find these final treasures?

- [ ] A drawing of the Jungle Queen
- [ ] Pictures of the crew
- [ ] An old radio
- [ ] A safari hat
- [ ] Two canteens
- [ ] Four oars
- [ ] Two wooden trunks held together with rope
- [ ] A pineapple
- [ ] A frying pan
- [ ] Red bullets
- [ ] A spoiled banana
- [ ] A mask featuring an elephant
- [ ] Someone's spilled cup
- [ ] A wrench
- [ ] A very long spoon

13. What do bullets, tusks, and wild animals have in common?

   a. They can all be found in art on the walls of the staging area.
   b. All are necessary items on the cargo list.
   c. They are all being used as playing pieces in a makeshift game of chess.
   d. They have nothing at all in common.

Adventureland Answers

Enchanted Tiki Room
1) a. Dole
2) d. Pineapple
3) a. Skilled
4) c. Both 'a' and 'b'
5) b. The sun god
6) b. Ngendei
7) c. Tangaroa-ru
8) a. Rongo
9) d. Maui
10) b. Maui
11) a. Tangaroa
12) c. Fish
13) c. Koro
14) a. Pele
15) b. From the limbs of Tangaroa
16) d. Pele
17) b. Hina Kuluua and Tangaroa-ru

Indiana Jones Adventure
1) d. The legend
2) f. All but 'c'
3) Yes
4) b. It's the license plate number of the Jeep.
5) b. High voltage
6) a. A triangle containing an eye

Temple View

7) c. Snakes

8) Collect 1 point per crumbled head _____

9) Yes

10) c. Tarzan yelling, monkeys shrieking, and elephants trumpeting

Inside The Temple

11) a. Water and treasure

12) b. It was covered with foliage.

13) d. Reports of the temple have hit the news.

14) Yes

Booby Trap

15) a. Loose rubble

16) Yes

17) a. The bats

18) c. Both

19) c. Sharp spikes

20) b. 2

21) d. A hat

22) a. Diamond

Large Temple Room

23) Total Treasures found _____

24) c. 2

Movie Room Pop Quiz

25) a. The Temple of the Forbidden Eye

26) c. The gates of doom

27) b. The globe

28) Yes

29) d. The riddle of the lost tourists

30) d. Tourists Lost in Temple

31) c. A skeleton

32) c. A chamber of destiny

33) b. A supernatural shopping spree

34) a. The safety belts

35) b. Looking into the eyes of the idol

36) d. All of the above

37) c. Who would win the World Series

38) a. That loved ones had disappeared inside

Jungle Cruise

1) a. There are five spears sticking out of it.

Jungle Cruise, cont'd.

2) c. 1911

3) b. Adventureland Dock

4) b. Crocodiles

5) Total Boat-Related Treasures found _____

6) c. Aero Eastern Motor Oil

7) c. Hyena

Booking Office

8) Total Booking-Office Treasures found _____

9) a. Travel agent

10) d. Our package tours

11) a. A boat

12) Total Office-Area Treasures found _____

13) c. They are all being used as playing pieces in a makeshift game of chess.

Critter Country

Davy Crockett's Explorer Canoes

Treasure Hunt Explorer Style: See if you can locate the following treasures before you climb aboard your canoe and paddle away:

- [ ] Bear claws
- [ ] A milk can
- [ ] A turtle
- [ ] Two crossed oars
- [ ] The name of the fort on the island
- [ ] A moose
- [ ] A cave
- [ ] A sun
- [ ] A pirate's crossed swords
- [ ] A crashed ship
- [ ] A barrel
- [ ] Two windows with no glass
- [ ] A fox
- [ ] A bell
- [ ] Two spyglasses perched on branches
- [ ] A small drum with feathers and beads
- [ ] A bridge

Splash Mountain

Outside Queue Entry

1. Treasure Hunt Time! See if you can locate these woodland treasures.

- ❏ A barrel up high
- ❏ Some water making itself useful
- ❏ An enormous wooden gear
- ❏ A source of light
- ❏ Roots
- ❏ A selection of crates
- ❏ A briar patch (sticky thorns)
- ❏ Some netting

2. Something doesn't look structurally right about the building with the water wheel. What is it?

a. The walls are crumbling.

b. The rooftop curves like a saddle.

c. The beams appear to have been lunch for termites.

d. The green paint needs redoing.

3. Welcome to Critter Country! What animal isn't welcoming visitors?

a. Bunny

b. Mouse

c. Turtle

d. Raccoon

4. One of the animals is displaying his shiny white teeth for you. Which one?

a. Wolf

b. Bear

c. Mouse

d. Fox

5. A sign offers you directions through Critter Country. Which of the following is missing from the sign?

    a. Davy Crockett's Explorer Canoes

    b. Splash Mountain

    c. The Many Adventures of Winnie the Pooh

    d. Hungry Bear Restaurant

6. A large old tree has a rustic carving of two bears having fun. What are they doing?

    a. They are trying to gnaw the tree down. (Maybe they are part beaver?)

    b. They are trying to push the tree over with their paws.

    c. One is sitting in the tree and one is peeking around it.

    d. They are hollowing out the tree to create a log boat.

7. There is a water fountain for the thirsty. What is it made of?

    a. Logs

    b. A waterfall that will get you wet right now

    c. A beehive

    d. Old rusted barrels

8. Look for an animal that always knows which way the wind is blowing. Which is it?

    a. Fox   b. Bear

    c. Squirrel   d. Mouse

9. Treasure Hunt Time! Find more woodland treasures.

    ❏   A place that used to be for wishing

    ❏   A garden arch that is not for the very tall

    ❏   A neighborhood for birds that are fond of red

    ❏   A stained-glass lantern

    ❏   Good advice for log boat riders

    ❏   A way to make things blow up

10. There is a door that tells you to stay out. But why?
   a. Big Splash production area
   b. Employees only
   c. Briar Patch seeding area
   d. Molasses vats

Storefront Area
You'll come to a storefront just before you enter the mountain. Take a close look and then see how many of these questions you can answer.

11. Is there a bear weather vane on top?
   Yes / No

12. Is there a bent pipe on the front?
   Yes / No

13. Is there a washboard?
   Yes / No

14. Is there a horseshoe?
   Yes / No

15. Is there a basket of apples?
   Yes / No

16. Is there a basket of eggs?
   Yes / No

17. Is there a bouquet of daises?
   Yes / No

18. Is there a pie safe?
   Yes / No

19. Is there a pitcher of lemonade?
   Yes / No

20. Are there four baskets of vegetables?
   Yes / No

21. Is there a U.S. flag?
    Yes / No

Tool Barn

22. Treasure Hunt Time! You have entered a tool barn. See how many of these dusty old treasures you can locate before you leave. **FP**

- ❏ A wooden rake
- ❏ Four chains
- ❏ A wooden shovel
- ❏ A milk jug
- ❏ A banister
- ❏ A wagon wheel
- ❏ A frayed rope
- ❏ A horse collar
- ❏ Some good luck
- ❏ A bucket
- ❏ A kettle
- ❏ An old rusty pitchfork
- ❏ Three big rocks
- ❏ A scythe (long handle with a curved blade on top)
- ❏ Three gears and a crank all hooked together

23. How many feet is the plunge ahead? **FP**
    a. 50
    b. Plunge, you say?
    c. 20
    d. 100

24. When did this tale happen? **FP**
    a. Yesterday
    b. The day before yesterday
    c. Long, long ago
    d. I'm not sure how long ago, but I think it was in a galaxy far, far away.

Lots To Do In Line Disneyland

25. What do you call a day where you can't open your mouth without a song jumping right out? **FP**

    a. A tra-la-la day

    b. A ZIP-a-dee-doo-dah day

    c. A day when other people look at you funny

    d. A magical day

A Good View

26. If you peek out the window, you will spot some critters near Splash Mountain. What are the bear and the fox holding? **FP**

    a. The fox has an apple and the bear has a wheelbarrow.

    b. The fox has a rabbit and the bear has some honey.

    c. The fox and the bear are holding their hats.

    d. The fox has an axe and the bear has a club.

27. The rabbit seems to be getting a free ride. How is he traveling? **FP**

    a. In the wheelbarrow

    b. Perched on the end of the bear's club

    c. On a kite; he's parasailing

    d. He is riding in the bear's pocket.

28. On the rock wall, there is something made from stone that is much bigger than it would be in real life. What is it? **FP**

    a. A rabbit   b. A carrot

    c. An acorn   d. A flower

29. What was true of the time when this tale was new? **FP**

    a. The critters were closer to the folks.

    b. The folks were closer to the critters.

    c. Things were better all around.

    d. All of the above

30. What will most folks not take the time to go looking for? *FP*
 a. The little critters' room
 b. Their laughin' place
 c. The briar patch
 d. Their own burrow

31. One Last Treasure Hunt! See how many of these treasures you can find before you get all wet. *FP*
 ❑ Three lanterns
 ❑ Three barn windows
 ❑ One pulley
 ❑ A beehive
 ❑ One red barrel
 ❑ One bridge
 ❑ Two tiny stone houses
 ❑ An unusual planter
 ❑ A rabbit wearing blue pants
 ❑ Windows that will keep you in
 ❑ A last chance for people afraid of water

The Many Adventures of Winnie the Pooh

As you walk under the sign for this ride, answer the following questions about Pooh and his friends.

1. What is spilling from the blue container held by Winnie the Pooh?
 a. Water
 b. Milk
 c. Chocolate
 d. Honey

2. Who is holding hands with Winnie the Pooh?
   a. Piglet   b. Tigger
   c. Roo   d. Eeyore

3. What is Roo putting a tack into?
   a. A message for Kanga
   b. Eeyore's tail
   c. A beehive
   d. A balloon

4. Who is upside down?
   a. Piglet   b. Roo
   c. Tigger   d. Winnie the Pooh

5. Treasure Hunt Time! See how many of the following treasures you can find before you have to buzz away.
   - ❑ A big red barrel
   - ❑ An animal with an elephant's head and a bee's behind
   - ❑ Seven carrots
   - ❑ A door covered in leaves
   - ❑ Two honey pots on their sides
   - ❑ Beehives (Collect 1 point for each hive you spot.) Total: _____
   - ❑ A house made of stone
   - ❑ A red birdhouse
   - ❑ A paw print
   - ❑ The sound of bees
   - ❑ A round window
   - ❑ A chimney
   - ❑ A clock
   - ❑ A cart

Critter Country Answers

Davy Crockett's Explorer Canoes
Total Treasures found _____

Splash Mountain
1) Total Treasures found _____
2) b. The rooftop curves like a saddle.
3) d. Raccoon
4) d. Fox
5) a. Davy Crockett's Explorer Canoes
6) c. One is sitting in the tree, one is peeking around it.
7) a. Logs
8) c. Squirrel
9) Total Treasures found _____
10) d. Molasses vats
Storefront Area (Answers 11 to 21)
11) Yes
12) Yes
13) No
14) No
15) Yes
16) Yes
17) Yes
18) Yes
19) No
20) Yes
21) Yes
Tool Barn (Answers 22 to 25)
22) Total Tool-Barn Treasures found _____
23) a. 50
24) c. Long, long ago
25) b. A ZIP-a-dee-doo-dah day
A Good View (Answers 26 to 28)
26) d. The fox has an axe and the bear has a club.
27) b. Perched on the end of the bear's club
28) c. An acorn
29) d. All of the above
30) b. Their laughin' place

Splash Mountain, cont'd.
31) Total Treasures found _____
The Many Adventures of Winnie the Pooh
1) d. Honey
2) a. Piglet
3) b. Eeyore's tail
4) c. Tigger
5) Total Treasures found _____

Disneyland Park Scavenger Hunt

You can hunt for the treasures below as you walk from attraction to attraction. Or if you prefer, you can devote part of the day to finding these treasures. Either way, keep your eyes open to rack up more points. Happy Hunting!

Adventureland

- ❏ A tiger eating a sign
- ❏ A mask with four swords crossed behind it that is displayed on a surfboard
- ❏ Oriental tattooing by Prof. Harper Goff
- ❏ A huge bunch of bananas with a net full of coconuts
- ❏ A blue peacock with its tail spread

Main Street, U.S.A.

- ❏ The phrase "a picture is worth a thousand words"
- ❏ The palm reader's shop
- ❏ Esmeralda
- ❏ A foot-massage machine

- ❑ A giant glass elephant
- ❑ A running model train
- ❑ A large Sleeping Beauty Castle inside a glass globe with balloons
- ❑ A hook and ladder
- ❑ An old-time Victrola
- ❑ The dental school
- ❑ A statue of Walt and Mickey
- ❑ A box where you can mail a letter

Tomorrowland

- ❑ An X-wing (as in *Star Wars*)
- ❑ A granite ball covered in water
- ❑ A driver's license photo spot
- ❑ Scout 207

Fantasyland

- ❑ A green zoo
- ❑ A timely performance
- ❑ A lighthouse
- ❑ People behind bars
- ❑ A large, sleepy sea mammal

Frontierland

- ❑ Horseshoe prints in the cement
- ❑ The home of the happiest horses on earth
- ❑ A flower-covered carriage
- ❑ A wanted poster for Alameda Slim
- ❑ A mine shaft that is all boarded up
- ❑ A mine shaft that opens onto a lake
- ❑ A cactus garden
- ❑ A fish plaque
- ❑ A wrecked shop gone aground

New Orleans Square

- ❑ A history of America's flags
- ❑ A petrified tree
- ❑ 33 Royal St.

New Orleans Square, cont'd.
- ❑ Jiminy Cricket looking through a magnifying glass

Critter Country
- ❑ A bear directing you to the restroom
- ❑ A little house all made of stone
- ❑ A beehive

Disneyland Park
Scavenger Hunt Tally

Total Treasures found _____

Disney California Adventure Park

Most of the challenges in California Adventure take place strictly in the lines. However, there are times when you will be wandering around the park from one place to another. Perhaps you need a break or want to find a good lunch spot. For those times, turn to the Disney California Adventure Park Scavenger Hunt at the end of this chapter.

Tip: You may want to read over the list now and then stay on the look-out. The treasures on the scavenger hunt list are scattered throughout the park. You get 1 point for every one you find.

Note: Unless specified otherwise, give yourself 1 point for each correct answer, 1 point for each Treasure you find, 1 point for each item you add to a Collection, and 1 point for any similar finds you make when you are hunting for something rather than answering a question. Good luck!

"a bug's land"

Flik's Flyers

1. What "flying" human creation is Flik using to make the sign for his ride?
   a. A tennis ball
   b. A toy parachute
   c. A paper airplane

2. Why did Flik create the Flik's Flyers machine?
   a. Because humans can't fly
   b. So all bugs would be equal
   c. Because ants can't fly
   d. Because flying bugs think they are sooooo special

3. As you came in you saw a picture of an ant taking a ride. What was he riding on?
   a. A dandelion gone to seed
   b. A leaf blowing in the breeze
   c. The back of a butterfly
   d. A propeller made from twigs and bark

4. Can you find any bugs that could fly without Flik's invention?
   Yes / No

5. Which of the following items of human trash did Flik use to create Flik's Flyers? Circle all correct answers.

    a. Chinese takeout carton

    b. A Jell-O box

    c. A pie pan

    d. An applesauce box

    e. A soup can

    f. A paper plate

    g. A whipping cream carton

    h. A pencil

    i. A raisin box

    j. An old cup

    k. A cookie carton

6. Flik also looked to nature when creating his flyer. Which of the following may be found on Flik's Flyer? (Circle all that are correct.)

    a. Dry leaves   b. Dry grass

    c. Moss   d. Vines

    e. Water   f. Twigs

    g. Flowers

7. What should you keep inside the flying machine at all times?

    a. Hands

    b. Hands, arms, feet, legs, what have you

    c. Hands and feet and especially antennae

    d. All parts that will not grow back

8. What would Flik like grown-ups to do?

    a. Hold on to your larva.

    b. Flap your arms for takeoff.

    c. Watch your kids.

9. Treasure Hunt Time! See how many of these things you can find before your blimp lifts off.

    ❑   Something that is 16 oz.

    ❑   A sun

    ❑   Something that was inspected by No. 2

- ❏ A blue curlicue
- ❏ A picture of two green leaves
- ❏ An apple
- ❏ Something that is 22 count per box
- ❏ A pagoda
- ❏ Writing in another language
- ❏ A pencil
- ❏ A straw
- ❏ A button
- ❏ A bar code

10. Still have some time left? Why not imagine how you would create your own flying machine for bugs from human trash and things in nature. You can draw your creation on the inside back cover of this book.

Francis' Ladybug Boogie

1. What has been used to create Francis' sign?
   a. A black donut   b. A tire
   c. A broken record   d. None of the above

2. The bugs have used everything they can find to create this tent. What item left over from lunch is part of the tent's structure?
   a. Straws   b. Paper bags
   c. Plastic forks   d. Part of a hamburger
                                      (Careful; you'll
                                      attract ants.)

3. What is the name of Francis' record?
   a. "Luck Be a Ladybug Tonight"
   b. "Francis' Ladybug Boogie"
   c. "Teeny Weeny Red Polka Dot Buggini"
   d. "He's No Lady"

4. What spins Francis?
    a. Bumping into other ladybugs
    b. The wheel in the middle
    c. Leaning to one side and then the other
    d. Nothing, he spins on his own.

5. Listen carefully. What do you hear all around you? How many unique bug sounds can you make out? (Give yourself 1 point for each individual insect sound you hear.) _____

6. How many spots are on each ladybug? Beauty marks do not count.
    a. 5   b. 6
    c. 7   d. 8

7. What does Francis want you to get ready to do?
    a. Boogie   b. Spin
    c. Dance   d. Rumble

8. What have the bugs used to create lanterns for Francis?
    a. Flowers   b. Cocoons
    c. Leaves   d. All of the above

9. Treasure Hunt Time! How many of these treasures can you find before you spin away?
    ❑   Six beauty spots
    ❑   Two straws with passengers
    ❑   Two musical notes
    ❑   Insect sounds
    ❑   Something yellow
    ❑   Something broken
    ❑   A large dessert

Heimlich's Chew Chew Train

1. Heimlich appears to have been munching on his Chew Chew Train sign. What meal was he indulging in when he ate some sign?

    a. Breakfast   b. Lunch

    c. Dinner   d. Dessert

2. Which of the following items can be found on Heimlich's sign? Circle all that are correct.

    a. Blue sprinkles

    b. Orange sprinkles

    c. Green sprinkles

    d. Red icing lettering

    e. A cherry

    f. A caterpillar

    g. Yellow sprinkles

    h. Pink sprinkles

    i. Chocolate sprinkles

    j. Whipped cream

    k. A missing bite

3. The wait-time sign is made out of what?

    a. A button

    b. An apple with a bite out of it

    c. A leaf

    d. A lollipop

4. Spot giant No. 2 pencils and earn 1 point for each one you find. _____

5. If you look over your head, you will discover that you are in a forest of sorts. What kind of forest is it?

    a. A forest of grass   b. A forest of trees

    c. A forest of clover   d. A forest of gumps

6. How many leaves does the clover in this forest have?
- a. 3-"But I'm lucky anyway; I'm at Disneyland!
- b. 4-"Bring on the good luck."
- c. 5-"Whoever heard of a five-leaf clover?"
- d. 3¾-"Now you are just talking crazy."

7. What creatures are providing light in this forest?
- a. Butterflies holding lanterns
- b. Fireflies
- c. Ants with a giant flashlight. "Those little guys are strong."
- d. Glowworms

8. What color are the wings of the fireflies?
- a. Some purple, some pink
- b. Some blue, some orange
- c. Some green, some red
- d. Some green, some purple

9. The fireflies are holding on to the clover with how many legs?
- a. 2
- b. 4
- c. 6
- d. 8

10. Heimlich appears to be eating again. What is he munching on now?
- a. Chocolate cake
- b. An orange slice
- c. Candy corn
- d. A leaf (Not likely with this caterpillar!)

11. What does Heimlich ask riders to do as he pulls out onto his path?
- a. Help him find something to eat
- b. Help eat all of his yummy treats
- c. Help find a place to nap off all of this food
- d. Help find his favorite food (His tummy is grumbling.)

12. Why do you think Heimlich is eating so much food?

    a. He is getting ready to become a butterfly.

    b. He is hungry.

    c. Both 'a' and 'b' are probably true.

    d. Heimlich is part pig.

It's Tough to be a Bug!

Outside Queue

1. Listen carefully to the small world around you. What things do you hear?

    a. A waterfall   b. Birds

    c. Music   d. A dog howling

    e. All of the above   f. All except 'd'

2. You have arrived at a stage for bugs. What is the name of this creepy crawly theater?

    a. Parasite Opera House

    b. Bugway Theater

    c. Honeywood Bee Theater

    d. Bug's Life Theater

3. The bugs that made this theater have been very innovative. What did they use to create the signs for their theater?

    a. Dried leaves tied on with vines

    b. Bits of cardboard boxes partially eaten away

    c. Butterflies spreading their wings as billboards

    d. Termites carved the letters into pieces of wood bark.

4. As you arrive at the theater, there is a rather rough looking bug waiting to greet you. What kind of insect do you think he is?

    a. A hornet

    b. A grasshopper

    c. A stinkbug

    d. A praying mantis

5. There is a warning to humans clearly displayed. What are we being alerted to?

    a. Constant clicking, strange smells, and holes in the ground

    b. Angry grasshoppers, sticky web curtains, and unsteady dung ball piles

    c. Loud noises, dense fog, and things that creep and crawl in the dark

6. Treasure Hunt Time! Can you find all of these items from the bug's world?

- ❑ Decorative pebbles held up by vines
- ❑ A windmill
- ❑ Two or more fists
- ❑ The word "Bye"
- ❑ Two exclamation points
- ❑ Princess Dot (She is an ant.)
- ❑ A string of leafy decorations
- ❑ A strong warning on a leaf

7. Locate as much wormwood as you can before you enter the theater. (Wormwood is wood with patches of wiggly lines eaten into it.)

    You get 1 point for each patch of wormwood you locate. _____

Inside Queue

Now that you are entering the cave, you will find posters featuring performers from today's presentation. Find the poster for Chili, the deadly Chilean Tarantula.

8. What kind of weapon have the flies created to battle the giant tarantula?
   a. A slingshot made of web and wood
   b. A cannon made of a hollow log and dung balls
   c. A sword made of an old plastic picnic knife
   d. A trap made of a box propped up on a stick

9. Whose act will you go nuts over?
   a. The Beatles' singing
   b. Harry Houfleani's magic
   c. Weevil Kneevil's acrobatics
   d. The Termite-ator

10. Who is creating a sign with bug spit? (Oooh! Gross!)
   a. Chili
   b. The Termite-ator
   c. The Dung Brothers
   d. Harry Houfleani

11. There is a stinkbug appearing in *It's Tough to be a Bug*. What is her name?
   a. Cindersmella
   b. Holdya Breath
   c. Ima Gas
   d. Claire De Room

12. Whose performance was reviewed by *Eaters Digest*?
   a. Flik's
   b. Chili
   c. The Beatles
   d. The Dung Brothers

13. You are about to enter the theater lobby. What special creatures do you see carved into the theater's name?
    a. Bugs, of course
    b. Butterflies
    c. Humans
    d. There is nothing carved into the name.

14. How many bugs star with Flik in *It's Tough to be a Bug!*?
    a. A million
    b. 5
    c. A million billion
    d. It is bad manners to count bugs.

15. Treasure Hunt Time! In the lobby, find these pieces of bug life:
    ❑   A bug using a napkin
    ❑   A sign that says "Hi Mom!"
    ❑   A magnifying glass
    ❑   A spotted leaf
    ❑   Five cockroaches with something to say
    ❑   An ant with a pet
    ❑   Three hourglass shapes
    ❑   A show that will "really bring the house down"
    ❑   Sawdust
    ❑   A rose
    ❑   A spotlight made from a flower
    ❑   Two dung balls
    ❑   Flik the ant
    ❑   Useful mushrooms
    ❑   A show declared a "Real Stinker"
    ❑   Someone who is a picky eater
    ❑   At least three leaf posters that appear unchewed

Tuck and Roll's Drive 'Em Buggies

1. Tuck and Roll are devastatingly handsome blue beetles. Look for them up front. What are they standing on?

    a. A record   b. A dung ball
    c. A tire   d. Each other

2. Tuck and Roll are holding a sign between them. How many bug limbs are holding the sign pole?

    a. 4   b. 6
    c. 7   d. 8

3. The tent containing the buggies has been festively decorated. Circle all of the decorations you see in the tent.

    a. A pink eraser
    b. Christmas lights
    c. A yellow crayon
    d. A thimble
    e. A leaf that's also a sign
    f. A plastic spoon
    g. A pink mirror
    h. Toenail clippers
    i. A lipstick
    j. A compact mirror

4. The crayons serve a function beyond decor. What else are they used for inside the tent?

    a. They guide traffic.
    b. They are used to keep score.
    c. They provide high up seating for bugs.
    d. Both 'a' and 'c'

5. What has been innovatively used as tent poles in this tent?
   - a. Clover
   - b. Twigs
   - c. Pixie sticks
   - d. Pencils

6. What are drivers advised to do?
   - a. Slip and slide
   - b. Spin and bump
   - c. Drive and crash
   - d. Tuck and roll

7. Who guarantees satisfaction?
   - a. Flik the ant
   - b. Tuck
   - c. Roll
   - d. P. T. Flea

8. Somewhere in the arena there is a leaf with something special about it. What is it?
   - a. It serves as a bug umbrella.
   - b. It has an arrow eaten into it.
   - c. It makes up part of the roof structure.
   - d. Tuck is wearing it as a jacket.

9. Treasure Hunt Time! See if you can find all of these bug treasures before it is your turn to roll away.
   - ❑ Someone in a spotlight
   - ❑ A Chinese food to-go carton
   - ❑ A yellow lollipop
   - ❑ A Q-tip
   - ❑ Two purple propellers
   - ❑ A leaf fan
   - ❑ A slice of watermelon
   - ❑ A green lollipop
   - ❑ A red-and-white umbrella
   - ❑ Three ladybug spots
   - ❑ A unibrow (two eyebrows that have become one long brow)
   - ❑ A candy corn
   - ❑ Corrugated cardboard (cardboard with ridges)
   - ❑ A blue hat
   - ❑ The words "Thank you"

- ❑ Moving bug blimps
- ❑ A big red belt
- ❑ Three people who crash their bug carts

"a bug's land" Answers

Flik's Flyers

1) c. A paper airplane
2) c. Because ants can't fly
3) a. A dandelion gone to seed
4) Yes
5) a. A Chinese takeout carton, c. A pie pan, d. An applesauce box, g. A whipping cream carton, i. A raisin box, k. A cookie carton
6) a. Dry leaves, b. Dry grass, d. Vines, f. Twigs, g. Flowers
7) b. Hands, arms, feet, legs, what have you
8) c. Watch your kids.
9) Total Treasures found _____

Francis' Ladybug Boogie

1) c. A broken record
2) a. Straws
3) d. "He's No Lady"
4) d. Nothing, he spins on his own.
5) Total Insect Sounds heard _____
6) b. 6
7) a. Boogie
8) c. Leaves
9) Total Treasures found _____

Heimlich's Chew Chew Train

1) d. Dessert
2) a. Blue sprinkles, c. Green sprinkles, d. Red icing lettering, f. A caterpillar, h. Pink sprinkles, k. A missing bite
3) a. A button
4) Total Giant #2 Pencils found _____

5) c. A forest of clover
6) a. 3; "But I'm lucky anyway; I'm at Disneyland!"
7) b. Fireflies
8) d. Some green, some purple
9) b. 4
10) c. Candy corn
11) a. Help him find something to eat
12 c. Both 'a' and 'b' are probably true.

It's Tough to be a Bug!
1) f. All except 'd'
2) d. Bug's Life Theater
3) a. Dried leaves tied on with vines
4) b. A grasshopper
5) c. Loud noises, dense fog, and things that creep and crawl in the dark
6) Total Treasures found _____
7) Total Wormwood Patches found _____
Inside Queue
8) a. A slingshot made of web and wood
9) c. Weevil Kneevil's acrobatics
10) b. The Termite-ator
11) d. Claire De Room
12) d. The Dung Brothers
13) a. Bugs, of course
14) c. A million billion
15) Total Lobby Treasures found _____

Tuck and Roll's Drive 'Em Buggies
1) c. A tire
2) b. 6
3) b. Christmas lights, c. A yellow crayon, e. A leaf that's also a sign, g. A pink mirror, j. A compact mirror
4) a. They guide traffic.
5) c. Pixie sticks
6) d. Tuck and roll
7) d. P. T. Flea
8) b. It has an arrow eaten into it.
9) Total Treasures found _____

Cars Land

Luigi's Flying Tires

Outside Queue

Welcome, welcome to Luigi's. Please come in. Your tires are looking a little road weary and Luigi has just the thing for you, flying tires. I am afraid a lot of customers are already lined up to try them though, so there'll be a bit of a wait for your test drive.

1. Luigi, he has quite an impressive Casa here, no? Look at the top of the building; it has tires built right onto the roof. How many are there?
    a. 6   b. 7
    c. 8   d. 10

2. They are very high up. Look around for evidence. How does it appear that they got up there?
    a. They are rubber; I expect they bounced.
    b. I think Luigi threw them up.
    c. This is where I get flying tires right? Perhaps they flew there.
    d. There are tread marks up the walls, so I am going to say they rolled up.

3. There is another decoration on the roof besides the tires. What is it?

    a. Italian flags

    b. Racing flags

    c. A Ferrari (a fancy car)

    d. Something besides tires? Surely not!

4. There is a wall where you can see many fine examples of Route 66 signs. Where else can you find Route 66?

    a. Painted on the street

    b. Adorning the gas pumps

    c. On a signpost

    d. All of the above

    e. Only 'a' and 'c'

5. What is on either side of the main entrance to Luigi's?

    a. Air stations; a tire is only as good as its air pressure.

    b. Tires, tires, tires; aren't they beautiful?

    c. A gas pump with an advertisement, "5 gallons free at Flo's with purchase of 4 tires."

    d. Nothing, Luigi, he would not clutter his driveway.

6. What is the brand of the tire you will be riding in?

    a. Lightyear

    b. Feather Lights Grande

    c. Fettuccini

    d. Rolling Stop

7. Treasure Hunt Time! See how many of these treasures you can find before they roll away.

    ❑   A small air pump with a crank

    ❑   Luigi, a yellow car

    ❑   1926

    ❑   A sun shape

- ❑ Cross ST
- ❑ Flame jobs
- ❑ A cement sphere
- ❑ The speed limit
- ❑ A tipping oil can
- ❑ A dinosaur

8. To go for a fly on Luigi's tires you must be at least 32" tall. There is a sign to check your height. What is it made of?
   a. A pile of tires. They can be useful for so much.
   b. A pole with a small tire on top. Everything's better with a tire.
   c. A stack of oil cans
   d. There's no height requirement for this ride.

9. In the window, there is a small clock. What does it tell you?
   a. When the shop owner will return from siesta
   b. The wait time from this point
   c. It's a clock, it tells me the time.
   d. That it is time for new tires

Inside the Tire Showroom
? **Pop Quiz!** There was a very big and impressive tower outside. Without looking back, see what you can remember about Luigi's fantastic tower.

10. It was made only of tires.
    True or False?

11. The tires were all lying down flat, one on top of the next.
    True or False?

12. There were strings of lights attached to the tower.
    True or False?

13. The tires were all the same size.
   True or False?

14. The tires were whitewalls.
   True or False?

15. The base of the tower was created using five very large tires.
   True or False?

16. The tires had hubcaps.
   True or False?

End of Pop Quiz

17. Ahh, you have entered the showroom. It is decorated to the most exacting standards. In many places, tires are featured in the design. Which of these sport tire décor?
   a. The columns. They are topped with tires; regal don't you think?
   b. The lights. They are shaped like tires; aren't they radiant?
   c. The railings. They are topped with tires; you don't think it's too much, no?
   d. All of the above
   e. Only 'a' and 'c'

18. What kind of car do you think Luigi prefers?
   a. Ferrari, definitely Ferrari. It is such a beautiful car.
   b. Fiat, it is Luigi's brand after all.
   c. Porsche
   d. Trucks of any kind

19. Which of these numbered cars is not fancied by Luigi?
   a. 12
   b. 24
   c. 36
   d. 74

20. Are there any racing cars with no number painted on their hood?
Yes / No

21. Look closely at the 24 Guigno Porto Corsa poster. There is something special about the architecture of the building and the landscape. Can you spot it?
Yes / No

22. Luigi, he carries many types of tires. Which of these tire brands is displayed in Luigi's showroom?
   a. Mostaccioli
   b. Tortellini
   b. Fettuccini. Hey wait a minute. Is this a tire showroom or a restaurant?
   d. Rotelle. Darn I am getting hungry!
   e. They are all on the menu…er, on display.
   f. Only 'b' and 'c'

23. There are also tires that are not named after pasta. Which of these brands of tires is not displayed in Luigi's showroom?
   a. Lightyear
   b. Glidewell
   c. Tred Star
   d. They are all there.
   e. All except 'c'

24. Do any of the tires on display have hubcaps featuring the Italian flag?
Yes / No

25. Are any of the tires wrapped up to keep them clean and safe?
Yes / No,

26. Are any whitewall tires on display?
Yes / No

27. It is always nice to know that you are dealing with an authorized dealer. What tire brand is Luigi an authorized dealer of?

a. Tred Star   b. Lightyear

c. Rotelle   d. Glidewell

28. Is there currently a sale at Luigi's?

Yes / No

29. If you are getting "tired," there is an impressive little parking lot in view just outside the window. What is parked there?

a. But of course, it is for cars.

b. It is extra-long truck parking for Flo's customers.

c. It is Luigi's VIP lot for Ferraris only.

d. How cute! It is parking for the bambinos' strollers.

Bulletin Board Room

30. How many racers are there in the Royal 400?

a. 17   b. 85

c. 200   d. 400

31. What country do you think the car pictured on the Royal 400 poster represents?

a. Italy   b. Japan

c. England   d. U.S.A.

32. Treasure Hunt Time! Luigi has four beautiful framed display boards of his life and travels. While you make a rolling stop, see how many of these racing treasures you can spot.

Frame One

❑ A horn

❑ A tuba

❑ A drum

❑ Italy

❑ Luigi's diploma

❑ The Popemobile

❏ Exhaust pipes in a knot
❏ A wrench

Frame Two

❏ A leaning tower of tires
❏ 20,000 Leaks Under the Sea
❏ The letter T made with bullhorns
❏ Floody Mary
❏ Motorama events
❏ A picture of Flo's
❏ Doc Hudson's autograph

Frame Three

❏ The Lugnut award
❏ Relief for a "hood ache"
❏ A Piston Cup
❏ Car #95
❏ Gask-its, Race Track Treat
❏ Lightning McQueen, with his tongue sticking out
❏ Vuvuzela, a plastic horn about two feet long
❏ Archeaological track specimens
❏ Antenna ornament
❏ Souvenir from the fastest pit stop ever

Frame Four

❏ A lion's tail where it should not be
❏ A real auto fan
❏ The sphinx
❏ A car with a bandaged eye
❏ The Eiffel Tower
❏ Bagpipes
❏ The world on wheels
❏ Luigi's pit-crew badges for races in Japan, Italy, and England
❏ A royal ride
❏ A 1st class ticket
❏ A winged lion

? Luigi's Office Pop Quiz!

Ahhh, You have arrived at Luigi's beautifully appointed office. Sadly, he does not seem to be in. Why don't you take a look around anyway? Luigi, he is a very friendly. You can see his office from inside and get another good look from outside. Look as long as you want. When you have looked long enough to know Luigi better than his own mamma, you can start answering.

33. On the wall was the logo for Luigi's favorite car. What animal was featured on the logo?
   a. Horse   b. Ram
   c. Jaguar   d. Hawk

34. His walls also featured a very useful table. What was it?
   a. Periodic Table of Elements
   b. Combustible Table of Elements
   c. The Complete Table of Pastas
   d. Automotive Table of the Elements

35. On the windowsill, there was a stand to hold a flag. What was in it?
   a. One Italian flag, one Japanese flag, and one English flag
   b. Three Italian flags
   c. One U.S. flag
   d. No flag was in the stand; the stand held a flower from Luigi's garden.

36. There was a toy car in the window.
   True or False?

37. There was an outstanding collection of bullet-shaped lug-nut covers displayed on the windowsill.
   True or False?

38. Whitewall tires were displayed under the window.
    True or False?

39. There was a drawer open on Luigi's desk.
    True or False?

40. There was a map over Luigi's desk. What did it show?
    a. Radiator Springs
    b. A street map for the World Grand Prix
    c. Italy
    d. There was no map.

41. Where does Luigi keep business cards he has collected?
    a. Pinned neatly to his wall
    b. Piled on his desk in a careful stack
    c. In a box currently sitting on his desk chair
    d. In the top right drawer of his desk

42. The clock in Luigi's office calls to mind cars. Why?
    a. It has the word Ferrari written across its face.
    b. It is shaped like a tire.
    c. The clock face looks like a speedometer.
    d. All of the above
    e. Both 'b' and 'c'

43. There was a calendar with a car in a red bikini on the wall.
    True or False?

44. There was a toy on Luigi's desk. What was it?

    a. An old-fashioned wooden car

    b. A red race car

    c. A plane

    d. A siren and flashing red light

45. Which of these things was stored safely under Luigi's desk?

    a. A tool box

    b. A whitewall tire

    c. A fancy tire rim

    d. A pile of name tags for tire displays

    e. All of the above; I think Luigi could use some storage cabinets.

    f. None of the above; Luigi, he is not that messy.

46. There was a big rubber floor mat just in front of the desk. What was pictured on the mat?

    a. A black stallion

    b. A red race car

    c. A Route 66 street sign

    d. A tire with wings

    e. None of the above, it was plain black rubber.

47. There was a framed certificate on the office wall. What was the certificate for?

    a. Passing a smog test

    b. It was Luigi's diploma from Tire U.

    c. A small-business license

    d. It was a certificate of appreciation for his work as the president of the Radiator Springs branch of the Ferrari fan club.

48. There was a stack of street signs in the office. True or False?

49. There was a small shelf on the wall. What was displayed on this shelf?

    a. Oil in cans and bottles. Perhaps Luigi will offer you a drink?

    b. The first tire he changed as a member of Lightning McQueen's pit crew. It was autographed.

    c. A collection of red model sports cars

    d. A collection of Ferrari swag, including several key chains and a license-plate frame that said, "My other car is a Ferrari"

End of Pop Quiz

In the Garden

50. Treasure Hunt Time! If you have any time left before you take flight, see how many of these treasures you can find in Luigi's garden.

- ☐ A gear
- ☐ A forklift on top of a pile of tires
- ☐ Leafy wheels
- ☐ A bear hard as a rock
- ☐ An air pump
- ☐ Cones full of light
- ☐ A planter with good traction
- ☐ A race car that has been parked so long it's becoming part of the garden
- ☐ A big red L

Mater's Junkyard Jamboree

? Pop Quiz!

As you pull up to this here jamboree, take a quick look at the sign above you. Don't stand there spinning your wheels for long though, you will create a traffic jam. Ready for the pop quiz? Park it here in line and see how much you remember.

1. What were the words "Mater's Junkyard Jamboree" written on?
   a. The tires
   b. A tractor
   c. The road beneath the tractor
   d. A trailer behind the tractor

2. How many tires were on the sign?
   a. 2
   b. 3
   c. 4
   d. Tires? No it was a hover vehicle, right?

3. The tires on the sign were spinning.
   True or False?

4. The tires were dressed-up a bit with rusty old hubcaps that did not match.
   True or False?

5. The tires were hanging from hooks.
   True or False?

6. The tires were completely bald (they had no tread).
   a. Yep, this is a junkyard after all.
   b. No, Mater would never allow that; bald tires are unsafe.

7. What was written on the tow truck?

    a. Mater Tows

    b. Call Mater when your junk really matters

    c. Tow Mater Towing and Salvage

    d. If you're stuck, Mater's your truck!

8. The word welcome is written on a choice piece of Mater's old junk. What is it?

    a. A tarnished hubcap

    b. A rusty old muffler

    c. A filthy license plate

    d. A warped street sign

9. What was in the trailer behind the tractor?

    a. A wooden crate   b. A pile of rusty junk

    c. A human rider   d. Flat old tires

End of Pop Quiz

Before the Junkyard

Look for the answers to questions 10 to 19 before you enter the junkyard.

10. My tires are getting a little tired. Where do you think I could park for the night?

    a. Ramone's paint and body; wake up freshly detailed for the road.

    b. The V8

    c. The Cozy Cone Motel

    d. Anywhere but at Mater's, I don't want to get towed.

11. Which of these special features does this rest stop boast?

    a. Free parking after 5 p.m. and on Sundays

    b. Automatic garage doors

    c. 100% Refrigerated Air

    d. Both 'a' and 'c'

    e. None of the above, it's a motel. Did you expect valet parking?

12. There is a garden with a water feature nearby. How pleasant. What is the water squirting out of?
   a. A fire hydrant
   b. A hose
   c. That's not a garden; it's a car wash. Good, I need a shower.
   d. A cone

13. Have a look at the big white building across the street from Mater's. What is its name?
   a. Ornament Valley Medical Clinic
   b. Ornament Valley Mechanical Clinic
   c. Ornament Valley Motor Care
   d. Now why would anyone put a white building in the middle of this dusty old desert?

14. Hey! There appears to have been an explosion. What exploded?
   a. An overfilled tire at Luigi's
   b. One of the pumps at the V8; I warned them not to carry high octane.
   c. Oh that, don't worry about it. It's just Mater backfiring again.
   d. A cannonball out of a cannon

15. What year was Radiator Springs established?
   a. 1909   b. 1926
   c. 1952   d. 1976

16. Mater offers special entertainment to kids while they wait. What is it?
   a. A junkyard playground
   b. A petting zoo
   c. A chalkboard wall for coloring
   d. A leaky old hose that sprinkles smaller guests with water.

17. Treasure Hunt Time! See how many of these treasures you can find before they rust away.

- ❑ Four peace symbols
- ❑ Organic Fuel
- ❑ A bunch of wheat
- ❑ A mailbox
- ❑ A U.S. flag
- ❑ A paintbrush with blue paint
- ❑ A water wheel
- ❑ A traffic light
- ❑ A sleeping car
- ❑ Two kinds of windmills
- ❑ A red fire hydrant
- ❑ A painted cactus

18. Look at Mater's collection of useless old rusty hubcaps. Impressive! Which of these things can't be found in the designs on these "treasures"?

a. Teeth   b. V8

c. Spokes   d. An eagle

e. Three shields   f. They are all there.

19. What is the significance of 5903?

a. It is the license plate number on a plate displayed on the poles holding up the tractor sign over the queue entrance.

b. It is the part number of an old engine resting under the hubcap display.

c. It is the address of the junkyard.

d. It was the mileage showing on Mater's dashboard display at the moment he first knew he wanted to be a tow truck when he grew up.

In The Junkyard

You are now entering Mater's junkyard. As you explore the yard and cruise toward the ride loading dock, you'll have the opportunity to earn lots of extra points by collecting license plates while you work on the other questions.

20. Extra Points!!! While you search for answers to the questions below, keep on the lookout for license plates. Each time you spot a plate from a new place, add it to your special license plate collection and give yourself 2 points.

21. Mater obviously has a taste for collecting. Piled on the ground all around you are some of his very favorite items. See how many of these parts you can spot rusting away on the ground.

- ❑ A propeller
- ❑ A stack of three bald tires
- ❑ Metal poles
- ❑ A large metal barrel on its side
- ❑ A tire with no hope of ever inflating again
- ❑ A muffler with two pipes coming out of one side
- ❑ A bumper
- ❑ An air hose
- ❑ A hood
- ❑ L-82
- ❑ A Chevy badge

22. Mater has a rather large slogan painted on the wall. What is it?

    a. If you can't drive with the monster trucks stay in the parking lot.

    b. You call, I tow, any questions?

    c. When the going gets tough, the tough get towing!

    d. Mater, Mater, he's our man; if he can't tow you no one can.

23. It appears that our friend Mater likes to participate in his community. He is a member of a group called the Mater Hawk. What is pictured on the Mater Hawk symbol?
   a. A tow truck with wings
   b. Three planes and one tow truck
   c. A tow truck with three birds perched on the top
   d. A tow truck flying a plane

24. He also participates in the local Rescue Squad. What is pictured on the Rescue Squad symbol?
   a. A tow truck and a police badge
   b. A police badge and a medical symbol
   c. A medical symbol and a fire
   d. A fire and a helicopter
   e. Wait a minute; those things are all there.
   f. They are all there except the helicopter; Radiator Springs is no place for someone with no wheels.

25. What is Skipper's?
   a. A fish restaurant: "Best clam chowder on Route 66, guaranteed!"
   b. A military surplus hut: "All American made, guaranteed!"
   c. A junk shop: "You want it, we've got it, guaranteed!"
   d. A flight school: "We can teach anyone how to fly, guaranteed!"

26. What does NASCA stand for?
   a. National Aeronautics and Space Coalition Administration
   b. National Association for Stock Car Auto Racing
   c. National Alliance for Stranded Car Assistance

d. National Automotive Space Car
Association

27. Treasure Hunt Time! You know the
expression "one man's trash is another man's
treasure"? See how much of this junkyard
treasure you can find before you move along.

- ❑ A fire hose
- ❑ An arrow-shaped street sign pointing at a hubcap
- ❑ Two license plates, one layered on top of the other
- ❑ Easy Idle
- ❑ The business part of a fan
- ❑ A jet with lightning wings, a helmet, and sunglasses
- ❑ A license plate with one letter different from the others
- ❑ A personalized vanity license plate from Mater's past
- ❑ No right turn
- ❑ Bull's-eye
- ❑ Moon Mater
- ❑ A window into one of Mater's past occupations
- ❑ A sign telling you to go "slow"
- ❑ Mater with a red cape
- ❑ A drum
- ❑ Wings
- ❑ A guitar
- ❑ A poster for monster truck wrestling
- ❑ Ice cream
- ❑ A paint stencil for the road at area 51.
- ❑ A crushed oil can
- ❑ Two checkered racing flags

? Pop Quiz!

Mater has never been one to let his engine idle for long. Think back to the junk you saw in his er...um...collection. Now see how many of these questions you can answer about the jobs Mater has tried.

28. In which profession did Mater use his bat wings?
    a. Heavy Metal band member
    b. Materdor
    c. Wrestler
    d. Astronaut

29. How were his wings affixed to his body?
    a. Rope
    b. Screws
    c. Hooks
    d. Duct tape

30. When Mater went by the name Tormentor, what was his job?
    a. Materdor
    b. Wrestling
    c. Rescue Squad member
    d. Heavy Metal band member

31. What was the name of Mater's band?
    a. Axel Tows
    b. Engine Block
    c. Mater and the Gas-Caps
    d. Twisted Fender

32. What was the name of the Tormentor's opponent?
    a. The Masked Love Bug
    b. Lave Los Llantas
    c. El Hook Dangerous
    d. Captain Collision

33. When Mater was a materdor, what did he fight?
   a. Bulldozers of course
   b. Tractors, he mostly liked to tip them
   c. A rather menacing looking threshing machine
   d. Not much, he just didn't have the drive for it.

34. What pieces of Mater's materdor ensemble were on display in the junkyard?
   a. Hood   b. Hubcaps
   c. Wheels   d. All of the above
   e. Only 'a' and 'b'

35. What evidence is there to suggest that Mater once was a private eye?
   a. An old newspaper clipping featuring Mater after he solved the case of the counterfeit tires.
   b. A window that says so
   c. A large magnifying glass with dashboard attachment
   d. Four tires with special "Ever Silent" tread for when you want to be sneaky

36. What was pictured in the center of the Rescue Squad badge?
   a. A police badge
   b. A fire
   c. A tow truck, Mater loves the spotlight.
   d. The initials RS for Radiator Springs

37. The junkyard evidence suggests Mater went to the moon.
   a. True, if I'm lyin', I'm cryin'.
   b. False, sounds like a tall tale to me.

38. The junkyard evidences suggests that Mater has underwater sub capabilities.
    a. If I'm lyin', I'm cryin'.
    b. Sounds like a tall tale to me.

39. The junkyard evidence suggests that Mater was once starred in the movie *Towmarow Never Dies*.
    a. If I'm lyin', I'm cryin'.
    b. Sounds like a tall tale to me.

40. The Junkyard evidence suggests that Mater was at one time a daredevil by the name of Mater the Greater.
    a. If I'm lyin', I'm cryin'.
    b. Sounds like a tall tale to me.

41. The junkyard evidence suggests that Mater may have in some way been mixed up with a secret government lab investigating extraterrestrials.
    a. If I'm lyin', I'm cryin'.
    b. Sounds like a tall tale to me.

42. The junkyard evidence suggests that Mater may have been an Olympic gold medalist in luge.
    a. If I'm lyin', I'm cryin'.
    b. Sounds like a tall tale to me.

Radiator Springs Racer

? **Entry Sign Pop Quiz!**

Glad you made it to the races. Today we are experiencing a bit of congestion on the road to the starting line, so now would be a good time to switch on the cruise control and check out the scenery. On your way in, you passed under a large gateway sign. Let's see what your onboard computer remembers about it.

1. The sign featured a big car. How many doors did it have?
    a. It was a two-door.
    b. It was a four-door.
    c. It had four doors plus a hatchback.
    d. It was a race car; you had to enter through the windows.

2. What words were written on the car?
    a. Radiator Springs Racers
    b. Ready! Set! Drive!
    c. Racers
    d. There were no words on the car itself.

3. What was the purpose of the wheels?
    a. FASTPASS Return Time
    b. Spinning and looking good
    c. Standby Wait Time
    d. I do not think you should be in a race if you do not know the purpose of wheels.
    e. Both 'a' and 'c'
    f. Both 'b' and 'c'

4. What did the sign say you were entering?
    a. Radiator Springs   b. Route 66
    c. The Radiator Springs leg of the World
       Grand Prix
    d. Ornament Valley

5. The car had eyes.
    True or False?

6. The car had a lightning shape painted on its side.
    True or False?

7. What were the words Radiator Springs constructed out of?
    a. A race track   b. Pipes
    c. Taillights   d. Asphalt

8. The posts holding up the gateway sign featured signs from local community-based organizations. Which of these was not there?
    a. The Knights of Combustion
    b. The Loyal Carhood of the Motor Heads
    c. Association of Cogs in the Machine
    d. The Loyal Order of the Lugnuts
    e. They are all there.

9. There was a racing flag on the sign.
    True or False?

End of Pop Quiz

10. The scenery is beautiful here in Ornament Valley. What are the initials out in the rocks?
    a. RS   b. WD
    c. OV   d. LM

11. Treasure Hunt Time! This drive can be quite scenic. Get your camera ready, keep your headlights shining, and get ready to hunt.
    ❏   A place for a lube

- ❑ An arrow pointing to a brick wall
- ❑ A boulder that looks very precarious
- ❑ The word motel
- ❑ A neon starburst
- ❑ A red fire hydrant
- ❑ Baked paint chips, yummy
- ❑ A Route 66 sign
- ❑ Yellow and red flags

The Road Ahead

12. Oh it looks like this race has a sponsor. What does RSN stand for?
    a. Radiator Springs Nonprofit
    b. Rolling Stop Nutworks
    c. Racing Sports Network
    d. Rust-eze Sportscar National

13. Why should you mind your speed?
    a. You could get a ticket.
    b. Tractor crossing, they're soooooo cute!
    c. You will be held accountable for road damage.
    d. The sheriff isn't slow.

Scenic Sign

This area has many natural wonders. Have a look at the Ornament Valley scenic sign to help you get the lay of the land.

14. What happens when a backup of pressurized exhaust escapes Pipe's Peak?
    a. The backfire rattles every window in Carburetor County.
    b. "Old Fuel-Injector" spews a fountain 20 feet into the air.
    c. Rocks move causing varying amounts of road damage. Proceed with caution!
    d. The resulting sound surge causes many cars to experience severe hood aches.

15. Which of the following is not an area shown on the Ornament Valley sign?
 a. Wheel Well Motel
 b. Lost Wheel Arch
 c. Firewall Falls
 d. Lost Cal Cave
 e. They are all there.

16. Where do wild tractors roam and John Deere play?
 a. Ranger Rover Plain
 b. At Double Clutch Gulch
 c. Carburetor Canyon
 d. Radiator Cap

17. Who discovered Radiator Springs?
 a. Mater, a tow truck who was attempting to haul a crashed extraterrestrial craft from the area. If I'm lyin', I'm cryin'.
 b. Homer, a road paver who was hired to help complete Route 66.
 c. Wilber, a tractor rancher whose tractors kept returning cool and refreshed.
 d. Stanley, a traveling radiator-cap salesman

18. There is a picture of Stanley. How wonderful. What is he doing?
 a. Filling his radiator at the spring
 b. Marrying his one true love, Lizzie
 c. Accepting a key to the city from Mayor Motor Mouth
 d. Handing out bottles of nature's finest coolant to a crowd of overheated fans

? **Pop Quiz!** I hope you had a good look at the Ornament Valley sign because we will now see how fast the wheels in your brain spin.

19. There was a mountain named Mount Ever Rust.
   True or False?

20. Most of the rocks were from the Automozoic period.
   True or False?

21. What was the name of the picturesque arch?
   a. Radial Tire Arch
   b. Rear window rock formation
   c. Lost Wheel Arch
   d. Half Hubcap natural bridge

22. Last Chance Gas Geysers are the final place to fill up a thirsty tank for over 100 miles.
   True or False?

23. How many waterfalls were displayed on the sign?
   a. 1
   b. 2
   c. 3
   d. No waterfalls, but there was a nice example of gasoline falls.

24. Which of these areas was identified on the scenic sign?
   a. Lincoln Continental Divide
   b. Radiator Cap
   c. Cars Bad Caverns
   d. Willys Butte
   e. All of the above
   f. All but 'd'

25. The Radiator River flows through the Grand Prix Canyon.
   True or False?

26. There was a picture of the inside of a cavern. What were the formations made from?
   a. Hood ornaments
   b. Taillights
   c. Rearview and sideview mirrors
   d. Dipping oil

27. What has Willys Butte been inspiring for years?
   a. Songs   b. Paintings
   c. Hood ornaments   d. Nature lovers

28. There was a very special cactus pictured on the far left of the sign. What was so unique about it?
   a. It was made of old tire tread with nails embedded in it.
   b. It formed the shape of a wheel.
   c. Part of it formed the shape of a car.
   d. It was in bloom with a taillight flower.
   e. Only 'a' and 'd'
   f. None of the above; it was just a regular old cactus.

End of Pop Quiz

Rusty Ridge Bridge

29. Now that you are familiar with the landscape here in Ornament Valley, you might enjoy seeing if you can locate some of the following in the actual landscape.
   ❑   Pipe's Peak
   ❑   Cadillac Range
   ❑   Radiator Cap
   ❑   Willys Butte

- ❏ Firewall Falls
- ❏ Mount Hood
- ❏ Lost Wheel Arch

30. According to the sign, what happens after one sip?
   a. You watch the miles melt away!
   b. Your engine starts humming with happy plumbing.
   c. You will be happy you did!
   d. Clinking and clunking will become a things of your past.

31. What is pictured with the words "Only Garage in a Mirage"?
   a. A sun, a palm tree, and wavy lines
   b. A car, a sun, and wavy lines
   c. A palm tree, a car, and a sun
   d. All of the above
   e. None of the above, just a garage door

32. What is available in all shapes?
   a. Mickey Mouse ears
   b. Souvenir hood ornaments
   c. Hubcaps
   d. Radiator caps

33. Where is there always gas?
   a. Stanley's, open 8 days a week
   b. Last Chance Gas Geysers, the final place to fill up a thirsty tank for over 100 miles
   c. Flo's in-canyon mini outpost
   d. Nowhere, but you can always call Tow Mater's; he will have some to you in a jiffy.

34. What is served ice cold?
   a. Natural gas
   b. Coolant smoothies
   c. Bottled oil
   d. Nothing; this is a desert, remember?

35. In what year was the Rusty Ridge Bridge erected?
- a. 1933
- b. 1947
- c. 1952
- d. 1960

36. You are about to see one of the great wonders of the world! Which one is it?
- a. 4.44
- b. 6th ish
- c. 8 ¾
- d. 100th I think

37. Wow, a wonder of the world. That's why this road is so congested! What is the wonder?
- a. A tire-shaped rainbow rock formation stuck in the mud
- b. A gasoline geyser called Old Bessie. It squirts gas in the air every five minutes.
- c. DoorHenge, a grouping of stones that resembles car doors mysteriously balanced on top of each other
- d. A natural rock formation in the shape of the front of a car featuring a spring

38. Is this formation Radiator Spring itself?
Yes / No

39. What year was the formation discovered?
- a. 1909
- b. 1928
- c. 1947
- d. 1966

Stanley's
40. You are coming to a store. What do you know about its hours?
- a. It is open every day except weekends, holidays, and when they don't feel like it.
- b. It is always open even when it is closed.
- c. It is usually open.
- d. It is never open; it's just a mirage.

41. What is free?
    a. A gas fill-up when a second fill-up of equal
       or lesser value has been purchased
    b. Fresh pressurized air for your road-weary
       tires
    c. The spring water, nature's very own fixer
       elixir
    d. Parking on Sundays and after 5 p.m.

42. What are the benefits of using Radiator
Spring water?
    a. Stops leaks
    b. Restores dull paint to original luster
    c. Cures road rash
    d. Soothes irritated brake pads
    e. All of the above
    f. All but 'c'; only time and lack of chafing
       will accomplish that.

43. If you wanted to top off with some cool
refreshing Radiator Spring water, where would
you get it?
    a. From inside the store
    b. I would drive right out into the spring and
       splash around till my tank was full.
    c. My engine is far too sensitive to take
       chances on free water. I get mine bottled.
    d. From the large dispenser pipes sticking out
       of the wall, naturally. Yum yum, wall water!

44. Which of these rules is true at Stanley's
Cap-n-Tap?
    a. If we don't have your cap, it is free!
    b. No exhausting indoors. Please only
       combust in designated areas outside.
    c. No tires, no fender skirt, no service
    d. They are all true.
    e. All but 'b'

45. Treasure Hunt Time! You are about to enter Stanley's Cap-n-Tap. Look around the store to see how many of these treasures you can find before you overheat.

- ❑ A square-shaped cap
- ❑ A pile of three boxes
- ❑ Something that costs 20 cents
- ❑ Old-time headlights
- ❑ A refill
- ❑ A cap with a long handle sticking off its edge
- ❑ A hood ornament
- ❑ A smiling drop of water
- ❑ A vale
- ❑ Speed limit of 50 mph
- ❑ A discarded tire
- ❑ A cap with a "X" across it
- ❑ A cap featuring lightning and a gear
- ❑ A red cap
- ❑ A cap that says 18 lbs
- ❑ A cap someone wrote on

Gas Station

As you exit Stanley's Tap-n-Cap you will enter a room with two very refreshing-looking gas pumps; just the place to be if your tank is feeling a little bit low.

46. Why should you come in for service?
   a. Because your wheels are tired
   b. Because your gauge is almost on empty
   c. Because you are "exhaust-ed"
   d. Well you are in a desert, and there is shade in there, sooooooo ...

47. What gas brand is sold here?
   a. Tulsa Tea   b. Butte Gas
   c. Dinoco   d. Flo's High Octane
                           Special

48. Take a look at the blue gas pump. What number is the indicator on right now?

    a. 0

    b. 1

    c. 5

    d. It appears to be broken. The indicator hands are hanging at the bottom.

49. The top of the gas pump pictures a famous landmark from Ornament Valley that you learned about earlier. What is its name?

    a. Radiator Cap   b. Mount Hood

    c. Cadillac Range   d. Willys Butte

50. This place has an impressive collection of old license plates. Which one has a cactus pictured on it?

    a. Arizona   b. New Mexico

    c. Nevada   d. Oklahoma

51. Which state has its flag pictured on the license plate?

    a. California   b. Rhode Island

    c. Texas   d. Wyoming

52. Find the license plate marked AW1-116. Where is it from?

    a. New Suspension   b. Torqueville

    c. Breakburn   d. Rollingstop

53. What state is the "show me" state?

    a. Washington   b. Missouri

    c. Georgia   d. Kansas

54. What state has a picture of the state itself on the plate?

    a. Kansas   b. Texas, and it's big, too

    c. Oklahoma   d. California

    e. Both 'b' and 'c'   f. Both 'b' and 'd'

55. What state's plate informs us that they are OK!
   a. California
   b. Oklahoma, where the wind comes sweeping down the plain
   c. North Dakota
   d. Mississippi

56. Treasure Hunt Time! If you are still in the second room, see how many of these car-fully chosen treasures you can spot.
   ❑ A car paint sprayer
   ❑ Wings
   ❑ Octagon
   ❑ A big blue R
   ❑ A star
   ❑ Self service
   ❑ Two ways to go
   ❑ A sphere with a gauge
   ❑ Dynalube

The Bottle House
57. What kinds of bottles were used to build this structure?
   a. Soda
   b. Water
   c. Oil
   d. Any bottle made of interesting colors

58. Stacked end-to-end, how high would the bottles used to make this structure reach?
   a. Higher than Route 66 is long
   b. Higher than the tallest fin of the Cadillac Mountain Range
   c. They would reach almost one hundred and twenty-six-thousandths the distance to the moon.
   d. I don't think you could balance those bottles end-on-end. Just saying.
   e. All of the above
   f. Only 'b' and 'c'

59. This building is made of a beautiful collection of bottles. Earn 1 point each (up to 3 points total) by finding a bottle by each of these manufacturers. Get 2 points extra if you find a bottle by a manufacturer that isn't listed. _____
   - ❑ CC Oil Co
   - ❑ DEX
   - ❑ GAW

60. From this room you can see race cars go by. Look for the different colors. Get 1 point for each color you find.
   - ❑ Dark blue
   - ❑ Baby blue
   - ❑ Aqua blue
   - ❑ Red
   - ❑ Burgundy
   - ❑ Green
   - ❑ Yellow
   - ❑ Purple

Last Leg of Your Journey
61. It is time to play "spotted on the highway." Have a look around at the traffic…er, I mean people…around you. You are trying to find the things listed below that are associated with cars. Earn 1 point for each one found. And remember, even cars hate to be pointed at.
   - ❑ Racing Stripes (a person wearing stripes)
   - ❑ Child-on-board sign (a child being carried by a parent)
   - ❑ Lowrider (a person who is jumping up and down)
   - ❑ Gas guzzler (a person who is drinking)
   - ❑ Tinted windows (a person wearing sunglasses)
   - ❑ Convertible (a person wearing a hoodie)
   - ❑ Visor (a person with a sun visor)

- ☐ Gray sedan (any two people who are dressed alike)
- ☐ Tail fin (a person with a ponytail)
- ☐ VW beetle (a person wearing neon)
- ☐ Forklift (a person eating)
- ☐ High clearance (a person taller than your dad)
- ☐ Ticket bait (a person talking on a cellphone)
- ☐ Spare tire (a person wearing a pouch)
- ☐ Car wax (a person wearing sparkly clothes)
- ☐ New paint job (a person with painted toenails)
- ☐ Doing donuts (a person spinning)
- ☐ Jack (a person wearing heels)
- ☐ Seat cover (a person wearing fur)
- ☐ New tires (a person wearing boots)
- ☐ Peeling paint (a person wearing multiple shirts)
- ☐ Antenna (a person with a balloon)
- ☐ Race flag (a person wearing black and white)
- ☐ Fuzzy dice (a person wearing spots)
- ☐ Air conditioning (a person fanning him or her self)
- ☐ Motorcycle (a child climbing on the railing)
- ☐ Bumper sticker (a person whose clothing features a brand name

Cars Land Answers

Luigi's Flying Tires
1) b. 7
2) d. They rolled up.
3) a. Italian flags
4) e. Only 'a' and 'c'
5) a. Air stations
6) c. Fettuccini
7) Total Treasures found _____
8) b. A pole with a small tire on top.
9) d. That it is time for new tires

Inside The Tire Showroom
10) True
11) False
12) True
13) False
14) False
15) True
16) False
17) d. All of the above
18) a. Ferrari
19) c. 36
20) Yes
21) Yes
22) f. Only 'b' and 'c'
23) d. They are all there.
24) No
25) Yes
26) Yes
27) b. Lightyear
28) Yes
29) d. It is parking for the bambinos' strollers.

Bulletin Board Room
30) a. 17
31) c. England
32) Total Frame Treasures found _____

Luigi's Office
33) a. Horse

Luigi's Flying Tires, cont'd.
34) d. Automotive Table of the Elements
35) b. Three Italian flags
36) False
37) True
38) True
39) False
40) c. Italy
41) a. Pinned neatly to his wall
42) e. Both 'b' and 'c'
43) False
44) b. A red race car
45) e. All of the above
46) d. A tire with wings
47) c. A small-business license
48) True
49) a. Oil in cans and bottles
In the Garden
50) Total Garden Treasures found _____

Mater's Junkyard Jamboree
Pop Quiz! (Questions 1 to 9)
1) d. A trailer behind the tractor
2) b. 3
3) False
4) False
5) True
6) a. Yep, this is a junkyard after all.
7) c. Tow Mater Towing and Salvage
8) b. A rusty old muffler
9) a. A wooden crate
Before the Junkyard
10) c. The Cozy Cone Motel
11) c. 100% Refrigerated Air
12) d. A cone
13) b. Ornament Valley Mechanical Clinic
14) d. A cannonball out of a cannon
15) a. 1909
16) b. A petting zoo
17) Total Treasures found _____
18) d. An eagle

19) a. It is the license plate number on a plate displayed on the poles holding up the tractor sign over the queue entrance.

In the Junkyard

20) Number of License Plates collected (2 points per plate) _____

21) Total Parts found _____

22) c. When the going gets tough, the tough get towing!

23) b. Three planes and one tow truck

24) e. Those things are all there.

25) d. A flight school

26) d. National Automotive Space Car Association

27) Total Treasures found _____

Pop Quiz! (Questions 28 to 42)

28) a. Heavy Metal band member

29) c. Hooks

30) b. Wrestling

31) c. Mater and the Gas-Caps

32) d. Captain Collision

33) a. Bulldozers

34) e. Only 'a' and 'b'

35) b. A window that says so

36) c. A tow truck

37) a. True, if I'm lyin', I'm cryin'.

38) b. Sounds like a tall tale to me.

39) b. Sounds like a tall tale to me.

40) a. If I'm lyin', I'm cryin'.

41) a. If I'm lyin', I'm cryin'.

42) b. Sounds like a tall tale to me.

Radiator Springs Racers

Entry Sign Pop Quiz (Questions 1 to 9)

1) a. It was a two-door.

2) c. Racers

3) e. Both 'a' and 'c'

4) d. Ornament Valley

5) True

6) False

7) b. Pipes

8) b. The Loyal Carhood of the Motor Heads

9) False

Radiator Springs Racers, cont'd.

10) a. RS

11) Total Treasures found _____

The Road Ahead

12) c. Racing Sports Network

13) d. The sheriff isn't slow.

Scenic Sign

*14) a. The backfire rattles every window in Carburetor
      County.*

15) e. They are all there.

16) b. At Double Clutch Gulch

17) d. Stanley

18) a. Filling his radiator at the spring

Pop Quiz (Questions 19 to 28)

19) True

20) True

21) c. Lost Wheel Arch

22) False

23) a. 1

24) e. All of the above

25) True

26) b. Taillights

27) c. Hood ornaments

28) c. Part of it formed the shape of a car.

Rusty Ridge Bridge

*29) Give yourself 1 point for each point of interest you
      tried to locate _____*

30) a. You watch the miles melt away!

31) b. A car, a sun, and wavy lines

32) d. Radiator caps

33) a. Stanley's, open 8 days a week

34) c. Bottled oil

35) b. 1947

36) c. 8 ¾

*37) d. A natural rock formation in the shape of the front
      of a car featuring a spring*

38) Yes

39) a. 1909

Stanley's

40) b. It is always open even when it is closed.

41) c. The spring water

42) e. All of the above
43) d. From the large dispenser pipes sticking out of the wall
44) e. All but 'b'
45) Total Treasures found _____

Gas Station
46) a. Because your wheels are tired
47) b. Butte Gas
48) a. 0
49) d. Willys Butte
50) a. Arizona
51) c. Texas
52) d. Rollingstop
53) b. Missouri
54) e. Both 'b' and 'c'
55) b. Oklahoma
56) Total Treasures found _____

The Bottle House
57) c. Oil
58) f. Only 'b' and 'c'
59) Points collected for bottle manufacturers _____
60) Total number of colors found _____
61) Number of people with car features found _____

Condor Flats

Soarin' Over California

Outside the Hangar

1. As you walked in you passed under a sign. There was a picture of something flying over a California coast. What was it?
    a. A bird
    b. A plane
    c. A helicopter
    d. A hang glider

2. There is a flight shop across from the queue. They sell something that's essential for take-off. What is it?
    a. Wings
    b. Gas
    c. Propellers
    d. Navigation systems

3. What fancy sign has been placed over painted lettering indicating a motor pool?
    a. Flight Shop
    b. Blast area - Keep clear
    c. Fly 'n' Buy
    d. FASTPASS Distribution

4. What kind of wax product is available at Flight Shop?
    a. Mickey's Wax
    b. Waxy Wax
    c. Quality Wax
    d. Ear Wax

5. The gas station has posted a sign requesting that you not do something. What do they want you to refrain from?
    a. Smoking
    b. Repairing vehicles in the lot
    c. Talking to the cars
    d. Climbing on the gas pumps

6. What three things top the flight tower?
    a. A weather vane, a windsock, and a green light
    b. A camera, a lightning rod, and a yellow light
    c. A windsock, an antenna, and a red light
    d. What flight tower?

7. You are visiting an air field. What is its name?
    a. Condor Flats Air Field
    b. Lucky Wing Air Field
    c. Radiator Springs Air Field
    d. Happy Landings Air Field

8. There is a large engine that blasts mist on the people below it. How many jets of "steam" come out of its blaster?
    a. 3   b. 4
    c. 5   d. 6

9. If you look around carefully, you will find someone advertising something pretty unbelievable. What is it?
    a. Over 100 billion served
    b. We will teach anyone to fly in one week.
    c. We repair anything in the air.
    d. 27 knives that can cut through a tin can for only $9.99

10. Something is soaring overhead. What is it?
    a. The Monorail   b. A model plane
    c. California?   d. A flock of seagulls

11. Treasure Hunt Time! See if you can find these high-flying treasures before you enter the building:

- ❑ A picture of Mickey Mouse
- ❑ A coiled hose
- ❑ Bubbles
- ❑ A parked airplane
- ❑ A car in the air
- ❑ Two each of red, yellow, and blue lights
- ❑ A wind sock
- ❑ A small red glider made of metal
- ❑ Three large yellow tanks
- ❑ Three red barrels with white stripes
- ❑ A latched yellow metal case
- ❑ A blast area
- ❑ A red light atop its own tower
- ❑ A steering wheel
- ❑ Three gauges
- ❑ A ladder
- ❑ A rocket test facility

Inside The Hangar

12. There are many photos of planes inside this hanger. Find one that pictures a plane with a checkerboard pattern on the top front of its fuselage. What is the name of this aircraft? **FP**

  a. Lockheed Vega

  b. P-51 Mustang

  c. Voyager

  d. F-80 Shooting Star

13. Find an aircraft whose crew is also pictured. **FP**

  a. Bell X-1

  b. F-80 Shooting Star

  c. The Douglas World Cruiser

  d. Space Shuttle Columbia

14. Find four planes pictured together. What is painted on each of their wings? **FP**

    a. BFFs 4 ever

    b. An arrow

    c. A peace symbol

    d. A star

15. Find a square-shaped plane with double wings. What year is it from? **FP**

    a. 1924   b. 1936

    c. 1947   d. 1958

16. Treasure Hunt Time! Find all of these flight-related items before you take to the sky. **FP**

- ❑ A plane's emergency exit
- ❑ A part with two very short arrows and one long one
- ❑ A decorative star
- ❑ The "Spirit of St. Louis"
- ❑ A DC3 from 1935
- ❑ Moving clouds
- ❑ Amelia Earhart
- ❑ Coils of orange and black electrical cord
- ❑ A man in a pinstriped suit and a bowler hat
- ❑ A "flying wing"
- ❑ The nose of a plane
- ❑ A plane's wing
- ❑ Draped chain
- ❑ An old travel trunk
- ❑ A giant propeller

17. What is the name of the mostly see-through plane built in 1977? **FP**

    a. Invisible Jet Plane

    b. The Gossamer Condor

    c. The Crystal Plane

    d. The Cloak

18. Who can boast of the West Coast?
   a. Howard Hughes
   b. Allan Lockheed
   c. Alys McKey
   d. I don't know. But boasting is rude, so I am
      not going to look.

19. Who was the first Chinese-American
woman to earn a flying license?
   a. Fu De Qu
   b. Alice Wong
   c. Lilly Chang
   d. Katherine Cheung

20. Treasure Hunt No. 2 Time! Look for a few
more flight-related treasures fast. They might
float away. *FP*
   ❏   A man wearing a leather flight jacket
        and helmet
   ❏   Chinese writing
   ❏   N803X
   ❏   Boards with lots of switches and gauges
   ❏   Speed limit 5 mph
   ❏   A builder of dreams
   ❏   The first black aviator to fly across the
        United States
   ❏   A man writing in a notebook

21. Circle all of the locations that you are to
soar over on today's flight. *FP*
   a.   Yellowstone Park
   b.   Monterey Bay
   c.   Miami Beach
   d.   Lake Tahoe
   e.   The Golden Gate Bridge
   f.   San Francisco
   g.   Washington, D.C.
   h.   Yosemite
   i.   The Everglades

j. Los Angeles
k. The Napa Valley
l. Mount Rushmore
m. Point Lobos
n. New York City
o. Redwood Creek
p. Palm Springs

Safety Video Quiz

Just before your flight you will be watching a safety video:

22. What must be stored under the seats? **FP**
    a. Hats, shoes, and magic wands
    b. Purses, cell phones, and any food or drink you smuggled in
    c. Cameras, purses, and Mickey Mouse ears
    d. Anything noisy, anything itchy, and well heck, put it all under there.

23. What must smaller aviators do if they don't measure up to the height indicator on their seat? **FP**
    a. Put the belt through the loop on the center strap
    b. Attach a parachute to their seat
    c. Request a roll of duct tape to securely affix themselves to the seat
    d. Ride in the under-seat compartment with the stuff they stashed

Condor Flats Answers

Soarin' Over California

1) d. A hang glider
2) b. Gas
3) c. Fly 'n' Buy
4) b. Waxy Wax
5) a. Smoking
6) c. A windsock, an antenna, and a red light
7) a. Condor Flats Air Field
8) b. 4
9) c. We repair anything in the air.
10) a. The Monorail
11) Total Outdoor Treasures found _____

Inside the Hangar

12) b. P-51 Mustang
13) d. Space Shuttle Columbia
14) d. A star
15) a. 1924
16) Total Treasures found _____
17) b. The Gossamer Condor
18) c. Alys McKey
19) d. Katherine Cheung
20) Total Hangar Treasures found _____
21) You will soar over: b. Monterey Bay, d. Lake Tahoe, e. The Golden Gate Bridge, f. San Francisco, h. Yosemite, j. Los Angeles, k. The Napa Valley, m. Point Lobos, o. Redwood Creek, p. Palm Springs

Safety Video Quiz

22) c. Cameras, purses, and Mickey Mouse ears
23) a. Put the belt through the loop on the center strap

Grizzly Peak

Grizzly River Run

Grizzly River Collections *FP*

1. Any time you are able to see the river rafts traveling below you, you can work on a special Grizzly River Collection or two. Here are some suggestions. How many of each can you find by the end of this line?

- ♦ People wearing plastic rain coverings ____
- ♦ People who are completely drenched ____
- ♦ Large aqua-colored containers ____
- ♦ Shovels ____
- ♦ Life vests ____
- ♦ Helmets ____
- ♦ Backpacks ____
- ♦ Sleeping bags or tent rolls ____

(Note To Parents: You may have to lift small children to give them a better look.)

❓ Big Bear Pop Quiz!
There's a big bear at the entrance. did you see him? I hope you looked closely.

2. That large bear was ready for some whitewater fun. What was the bear bringing on his adventure?

    a. A life vest, a helmet, a parachute, a fishing rod, and a wooden boat

    b. A helmet, a flashlight, a paddle, a lunchbox, and a canoe

    c. A helmet, a lantern, a paddle, a life vest, and an inflatable raft

    d. A fishing hat, a fishing rod, a tackle box, and an inflatable raft

3. That bear sported some very large teeth. How many teeth were protruding from his happy mouth?

    a. 2   b. 3

    c. 4   d. He had a full set of teeth.

4. The sign for this ride included something you will see lots of as you wait in this queue. What was it?

    a. An oar   b. A raft

    c. A bucket   d. A life vest

5. A signpost with an arrow directed FASTPASS traffic. What was the signpost made from?

    a. A shovel

    b. An oar

    c. A rusty chain stretched from the roof to the floor

    d. A canoe

6. There was a red lantern. Where was it?

    a. Perched in the branches of a tree

    b. Balanced on top of a stack of three crates

    c. Hanging from an oar suspended from the ceiling

    d. Hanging between the Standby and FASTPASS entrances

7. What was the significance of the number 42?
   a. It was the number on the canoe hanging overhead.
   b. It was the number of rafts available on this ride.
   c. It was the number of oars you could find between there and the boarding area.
   d. It was the height you must be in inches to enjoy this ride.
   e. Both 'a' and 'd'
   f. All of the above

End of Pop Quiz

Queue Entry

8. There is a sign to check your height before you are allowed to take this whitewater rafting trip. What is it made of?
   a. A pipe, part of an oar, and some rope
   b. A stack of life vests
   c. An oar stuck in a pot full of rocks
   d. A crate. If you are not taller than it is, you can't ride.

9. You will pass a warning sign. What ominous fact does it provide?
   a. "You will get wet, and you will spin. Let's just hope you don't fall in!"
   b. "You may enter dry, but you won't leave that way!"
   c. "You will get wet; you may get soaked!"
   d. "Did you bring spare clothes?!"

10. Treasure Hunt Time! Try to find some of these water-worthy treasures before you climb aboard your raft:
   ❑ An oar tied securely to a wooden pole
   ❑ A red life vest up high
   ❑ A helmet
   ❑ A Carabineer

- ☐ A pan
- ☐ Metal wheels for pulling heavy loads on a pole
- ☐ A green lamp
- ☐ A waterfall
- ☐ Two large discarded gears

Tip: This is a good area to look for some of the special Collections found only in this ride. See page 200 for the list.

Office Area

11. What has a picture of a pinecone and pine needles?

    a. The oars
    b. The trash cans
    c. The canoes
    d. The life vests worn by the ride personnel

12. You have come to an office area. Which of the following things is not in the office?

    a. A banana   b. A spoon
    c. A stump   d. Old-style
                                  headphones

13. This office is stocked with some unusual things. Which of these items can you find in it?

    a. A bee smoker
    b. A compass
    c. A foot air pump
    d. They are all there.
    e. They are all there except 'c.'

14. You will also find some more standard office supplies here. Which ones?

    a. A three-hole punch
    b. A pencil sharpener
    c. A cup full of pens
    d. All three.
    e. All except 'c'

15. Repair Shop Treasure Hunt! Can you find:
   - ❑ A saw
   - ❑ A wooden mallet
   - ❑ A fan
   - ❑ A stump
   - ❑ A paintbrush
   - ❑ Something that is upside-down
   - ❑ A lantern
   - ❑ At least four clamps (two wood and two metal)
   - ❑ A carpenter's plane for woodworking
   - ❑ A thermos
   - ❑ A cup of coffee
   - ❑ A rusty chain
   - ❑ A red-and-white-striped triangle
   - ❑ An anvil
   - ❑ A combination lamp and hook
   - ❑ An oil can

16. What note was left on the chalkboard about the recent trip in boat No. 2 to Old Scary?
   a. "I saw a ghost! Have you seen that thing?"
   b. "It's doing it again."
   c. "Don't go there!"
   d. "Why would anyone travel to Old Scary?"

? Office Pop Quiz!

As you pass by the office again on the other side, take one more really good look before turning your back on it. Circle Y (Yes) if you think a thing was in the office and N (No) if it wasn't.

17. *Life* magazine Y / N
18. A lunch box Y / N
19. A first-aid kit Y / N
20. A model car Y / N
21. A staple remover Y / N
22. Two hard hats Y / N
23. A sewing kit Y / N

24. One ranger hat Y / N
25. A telephone Y / N
26. A thermos Y / N
27. Two canoes Y / N
28. An outlet Y / N
29. A picture of Mickey Mouse Y / N
30. A magnifying glass Y / N
31. Two fishing baskets Y / N
32. A three-ring binder Y / N
33. A bug collection Y / N

End of Pop Quiz

After the Office

34. You will now pass by a good place for viewing the passing rafts. They are each numbered. Try to collect all of the numbers 0 through 9. As you find them, cross them off the list. **FP**

0 1 2 3 4 5 6 7 8 9

Note: As you pass the next area you will have a good view of the river. Remember to check the passing rafts for the Collections you'll find only on this ride (see page 200).

35. What company's buildings are right in front of the launch point?
    a. M.M. & D.D Inc.
    b. W.D. Rafting Inc.
    c. White Water Adventures Unlimited
    d. Eureka Gold and Timber Company

36. Can you find a wind chime made from old parts?
    Yes/No

37. Some things are being stored on a corner ledge. What are they?
   a. Three metal barrels in two colors and a pile of chopped wood
   b. Four metal barrels in three colors and a strange machine with three prominent gears
   c. A large pile of buckets and a broken canoe
   d. A pile of oars, and a crate marked "Waterproof Mickey Mouse Dolls"

38. Which of the following things is not on these buildings?
   a. A pile of rusty pipes
   b. An antenna
   c. A hanging bucket
   d. A broken ladder
   e. They are all there.

39. Can you point out something gigantic that you would never want to fall on you?
   Yes/No
   What is it? (*Hint:* One has fallen down.)

40. A giant saw-wheel is being used in a new way. How? **FP**
   a. As a frame for a photo
   b. As a picnic table
   c. As a warning sign
   d. As a roof

41. You will pass under one more water warning. What is it? **FP**
   a. Buckets
   b. Dripping pipes
   c. Wet clothes on an overhead clothesline
   d. Both 'a' and 'c'

In the last few seconds before you drift off in your raft, I suggest you put this book somewhere dry, for soon you'll be wet!

Redwood Creek Challenge Trail Scavenger Hunt

1. **Animal Tracking Challenge**

   Scattered throughout Redwood Creek are signs telling you about different animals you might expect to encounter in the redwood forests of California. The signs even show you what each animal's foot- or pawprint ("track") looks like. Those silly animals ran all over the place before the sidewalk cement was dry, leaving lots of tracks. Can you find each animal's sign and track?

   Award yourself 1 point for each animal's sign you find and another point for each track you spot.

   Striped skunk: sign __ track __
   Black bear: sign __ track __
   River otter: sign __ track __
   Bighorn sheep: sign __ track __
   Yellow-bellied marmot: sign __ track __
   Coyote: sign __ track __
   Tule elk: sign __ track __
   California quail: sign __ track __
   Porcupine: sign __ track __
   Beaver: sign __ track __

Scavenger Hunt

2. What happened in 818 A.D.?

   a. The first wooly mammoth walked the earth.

   b. The Millennium sequoia tree sprouted.

   c. Big Sur was first discovered and named.

   d. Disneyland Park first opened its doors.

3. Who is creating a fire hazard by roasting marshmallows?
   a. A skunk who does not look like he was trained for it
   b. One of the park rangers (I wonder if he will share?)
   c. A rather nervy bear
   d. Don't know; the fire is unattended.

4. Who can prevent forest fires?
   a. Only you
   b. Smokey the Bear
   c. Water

5. What should you not touch or feed?
   a. Any of the live animals
   b. The moose
   c. The bears
   d. The sleeping baby in that stroller over there

6. Oh, no. I see a sign for a rock slide. What is coming down the rock wall?
   a. Rocks, of course (Didn't you read that sign?)
   b. Water (I wonder how they got that sign wrong?)
   c. Me! It's my turn!

Animal Statue Area

When you visit the animal statues, find the answers to the following questions:

7. What is an indication that you will always be calm, cool, and true?
   a. Whenever a dragonfly lands upon you
   b. Whenever a mouse lives in your house
   c. If you can sing in harmony with the frogs
   d. If you can last though the line for Toy Story Mania! without asking, "Are we there yet?"

8. Whose prideful gobbling of the moon caused the widening of every frog's mouth?
    a. Tol'-Le-Loo
    b. Welketi
    c. 'Ase
    d. I met a guy with a big mouth once; I wonder if it could be his fault.

9. Who is a musical healer?
    a. A child
    b. Welketi
    c. 'Ase
    d. Both 'a' and 'c'
    e. All three; it was a group effort.

10. Who is the fire thief?
    a. Tol'-Le-Loo
    b. 'Ase
    c. Welketi
    d. Some kid with the last name Jackson. No, wait. That's lightning.

11. Why was coyote swallowed bit by bit?
    a. The bear's tail he had bit.
    b. He was howling and would not sit.
    c. He fell into a lion's pit.
    d. He was taunting the wrong fish and would not quit.

12. Why did raven smear himself black?
    a. So he could hide in a hole when he wanted to cack.
    b. So his prey wouldn't see him when he swooped to attack.
    c. So his wings would blend in when laid on his back.
    d. So he'd look like his friends and avoid any flack.

13. Who protects the Sun even when he sleeps?
   a. Ah-wahn'-dah
   b. Welketi
   c. Tol'-Le-Loo
   d. 'Ase

14. Treasure Hunt Time! Try to find all of these cool nature treasures while you enjoy the Redwood Creek Challenge area.
   ☐ A tree that was hit by lightning
   ☐ A ride that most grown-ups are not permitted on
   ☐ A place where you may get wet
   ☐ An old piece of radio equipment
   ☐ A way to get a close-up look at nature.
   ☐ A wooly mammoth with a broken tusk
   ☐ A place with netting all around you except on top
   ☐ Some native gold
   ☐ A first-aid trunk
   ☐ A ranger hat that is not atop a head
   ☐ A microphone
   ☐ A magnifying glass
   ☐ A real pine cone
   ☐ Snowshoes
   ☐ Four shovels
   ☐ A tree you can walk through
   ☐ A cardinal
   ☐ A skeleton of a snake
   ☐ Headphones
   ☐ Three bears holding so still they could be made of rock
   ☐ A hieroglyph of the sun
   ☐ A spirit animal all your own
   ☐ An eagle hieroglyph
   ☐ A battle between bear and fish (This is a hard one.)
   ☐ Animal sounds

Grizzly Peak Answers

Grizzly River Run

1) *Number of items collected* _____

Big Bear Pop Quiz (Answers 2 to 7)

2) c. A helmet, a lantern, a paddle, a life vest, and an inflatable raft

3) c. 4

4) a. An oar

5) b. An oar

6) d. Hanging between the Standby and FASTPASS entrances

7) e. Both 'a' and 'd'

Queue Entry

8) a. A pipe, part of an oar, and some rope

9) c. "You will get wet; you may get soaked!"

10) *Total Treasures found* _____

Office Area

11) b. The trash cans

12) a. A banana

13) d. They are all there.

14) e. All except 'c'

15) *Total Repair Shop Treasures found* _____

16) c. "Don't go there!"

Office Pop Quiz (Answers 17 to 33)

17) Yes

18) Yes

19) Yes

20) No

21) Yes

22) Yes

23) No

24) Yes

25) Yes

26) Yes

27) Yes

28) Yes

29) No

30) No

31) Yes

32) No
33) No
After the Office
34) Total Numbers crossed off _____
35) d. Eureka Gold and Timber Company
36) Yes
37) b. Four metal barrels in three colors and a strange
    machine with three prominent gears
38) a. A pile of rusty pipes
39) Yes; two huge metal barrels
40) c. As a warning sign
41) a. Buckets

Redwood Creek Challenge Trail
Animal Tracking
1.a.) Total Animal Signs found _____
1.b.) Total Animal Tracks found _____
Scavenger Hunt
2) b. The Millennium sequoia tree sprouted.
3) c. A rather nervy bear
4) a. Only you
5) b. The moose
6) c. Me! It's my turn!
Animal Statue Area (Answers 7 to 13)
7) a. Whenever a dragonfly lands upon you
8) b. Welketi
9) c. 'Ase
10) a. Tol'-Le-Loo
11) d. He was taunting the wrong fish and would not quit.
12) b. So his prey wouldn't see him when he swooped to
    attack.
13) a. Ah-wahn'-dah
14) Total Treasures found _____

Hollywood Land

Disney Animation

Disney Animation is a unique activity. Here the attractions and the waits meld together for Animation Academy, Character Close-up, and Sorcerer's Workshop because the waiting area for these attractions is filled with Disney movie magic and sound. It would take away from your experience to do anything but simply enjoy them. One Exception:

The small waiting area
for Turtle Talk with Crush

1. If you find youself waiting for Crush, you may want to see how many of these underwater treasures you can find before you start talking to strange turtles:

- ❑ A small orange fish
- ❑ A long skinny coral with openings in the ends
- ❑ Seaweed forming an arch
- ❑ A black and yellow fish
- ❑ A pink and yellow fish
- ❑ Sand

- ❑ Coral that looks like a bush that has lost all of its leaves
- ❑ A plant that looks like very long grass
- ❑ Pink coral with circles all over it
- ❑ A thorny-looking coral

2. Work on one of your Collections if you run out of Treasures to find. Sparkling shoes, shoes with no laces, and funny backpacks would all work well here. See page 13 for additional suggestions.

Disney Junior—Live On Stage!

1. Look around the theater. There are two fancy creatures made of gold. What kind of animals are they?

a. Giraffes   b. Horses
c. Elephants   d. Bears

2. What do these animal friends of ours seem to be doing?

a. They are sitting on top of tall poles.
b. They are riding bicycles.
c. They are signing autographs and posing for pictures.
d. All of the above

3. The elephants seem to be resting on a platform. Can you see another animal pictured on the platform? Look carefully. What animal is it?

a. A fish   b. A cow
c. A horse   d. A lion

4. Treasure Hunt Time! See how many of these treasures you can find before the pre-show video starts.

- ❏ A train
- ❏ A parrot
- ❏ A bridge
- ❏ A zigzag rooftop
- ❏ A gold ball with three rings around it
- ❏ A large gold hotdog
- ❏ Blocks with letters on them
- ❏ A bush trimmed to look like a rectangle
- ❏ A drink wearing sunglasses
- ❏ A saw
- ❏ A Mickey Mouse head
- ❏ A lot of light bulbs
- ❏ A very small green person
- ❏ A palm tree
- ❏ Flower decorations on a building
- ❏ A sword

5. Disney is a bright and colorful place. Try to find something around you in each of these colors, and give yourself one point for each color you find.

- ❏ Red
- ❏ Blue
- ❏ Green
- ❏ Yellow
- ❏ Orange
- ❏ Pink
- ❏ Purple
- ❏ Brown
- ❏ Black
- ❏ White
- ❏ Gold
- ❏ Silver

6. For anyone age 6 and under: Here's a chance to earn some bonus points. Listen carefully. If there is music playing, you can earn 3 bonus points for your best dance.

Hyperion Theater Memory Games

? Pop Quizzes!

As you head to the waiting area you will pass several large theatrical billboards. Stop and check out as many of them as you want to try to remember. Take a good look at them. Then move on to the end of the line and see how many questions you can answer without looking back.

Moon Over Monrovia Billboard

1. What Disney stars were featured in this poster?
   a. Mickey and Minnie
   b. Donald and Daisy
   c. Goofy and Chip 'n Dale
   d. The Little Einsteins

2. Someone was taking a nap. Who was it?
   a. The Moon   b. Donald
   c. Mickey   d. A toy solder

3. What did the billboard say life is?
   a. Musical   b. Colorful
   c. Tropical   d. Ducky

4. What was the toy soldier doing?
   a. Sleeping   b. Marching
   c. Making music   d. Dancing

5. How many pink bows were in the picture?
   a. None
   b. 1
   c. 2
   d. 3

6. How many musical notes were in the picture?
   a. 1
   b. 2
   c. 3
   d. 4

7. What animals, aside from ducks, were in this picture?
   a. Elephants
   b. Mice
   c. Lions
   d. This was a duck-only picture.

8. Daisy was sporting some lovely pink heels for her night out. What was Donald wearing on his, um, feet?
   a. Shiny black shoes
   b. Nothing
   c. Tennis shoes
   d. Red tap shoes

9. There was a building in the picture. What kind of building was it?
   a. A skyscraper
   b. A restaurant
   c. A house
   d. That was a car, not a building.

10. Was Daisy wearing any jewelry?
   a. Yes, she had a diamond ring.
   b. Yes, she was wearing a necklace.
   c. Yes, she had on a bracelet.
   d. No, ducks rarely wear jewelry.

11. What were our duck friends wearing on their heads?
   a. A tiara and a silk hat
   b. A bow and a top hat
   c. A feathered hat and a baseball cap
   d. Nothing of course, these are ducks we're talking about.

12. Were the ducks holding hands?
   Yes / No

Down Catalina Way Billboard

1. What famous Disney stars were featured on this billboard?
   a. Mickey and Minnie
   b. Donald and Daisy
   c. Goofy and Chip 'n Dale
   d. The Little Einsteins

2. Which of the following types of fruit were not featured on Minnie's very tropical headwear?
   a. Pineapple   b. Red apple
   c. Orange   d. Green grapes

3. How many bananas was Minnie wearing?
   a. 3   b. 4
   c. 5   d. There were bananas?

4. There was a building in the background. What color was it?
   a. Red   b. Pink
   c. Orange   d. Green

5. There was an unexpected creature in this picture. What was it?
   a. A flying fish
   b. A unicorn
   c. A dragon
   d. A porcupine

6. What was Mickey doing?
   a. Holding Minnie's hand
   b. Singing
   c. Dancing
   d. Kissing Minnie

7. What was Mickey wearing?
   a. A cap   b. A fur coat
   c. A tuxedo   d. A vest

8. What was Minnie wearing?
   a. A fluffy skirt and a tube top
   b. A tight wrap dress and high heels
   c. A ball gown with enormous puffy sleeves
   d. A bikini with pink polka dots

9. What celestial objects could be seen in the picture?
   a. Planets   b. The moon
   c. Stars   d. All of the above
   e. All except 'c'

10. What color was the band around Mickey's hat?
    a. Orange   b. Green
    c. Blue   d. Pink

11. How many bracelets was Minnie wearing?
    a. None   b. 1
    c. 3   d. 4

12. Was there a bird in the picture?
    a. Yes, a toucan
    b. Yes, a parrot
    c. Yes, two lovebirds
    d. No birds there.

13. Were there any lights in the picture?
    a. Yes, a lava lamp
    b. Yes, searchlights
    c. Yes, a spotlight
    d. No, it was a poorly lit picture.

14. The billboard told you that *Down Catalina Way* was exploding with new songs and dances. How many were there?

    a. 2   b. 5

    c. 7   d. 10

15. Were there any musical notes in the picture?
Yes / No

Hollywood Pictures
Cinetone News Billboard

1. How many cameramen were in the picture?

    a. None   b. 1

    c. 2   d. 3

2. What was on the head of the cameraman or men?

    a. A backward hat

    b. Mickey Mouse ears

    c. A scarf

    d. Hair

3. One famous Disney character appeared on this billboard. Who was it?

    a. Minnie   b. Donald

    c. Mickey   d. Goofy

Did this billboard feature:

4. A train?
Yes / No

5. An airplane?
Yes / No

6. A sailing ship?
Yes / No

7. A helicopter?
Yes / No

8. A tank?
   Yes / No

9. A horse and buggy?
   Yes / No

10. An old-fashioned car?
    Yes / No

11. How many people were in the picture?
    a. 2   b. 3
    c. 9   d. A huge crowd

12. What was the biggest, most prominent word on the billboard?
    a. Hollywood
    b. News
    c. Cinetone
    d. All the words were the same size.

13. There was a motorcycle. Was someone on it?
    Yes / No

On the Great Stage Billboard

There was a woman jumping in the picture. Which of the following things are true about her?

(Circle all that are correct.)

1. She was wearing a green vest.
   Yes / No

2. She had bare feet.
   Yes / No

3. She had short hair.
   Yes / No

4. She was playing the cymbals.
   Yes / No

5. She was playing a trombone.
   Yes / No

6. She was wearing earrings.
   Yes / No

7. She was wearing anklets.
   Yes / No

8. She was wearing a short one-piece dress.
   Yes / No

End of questions about the jumping woman

9. Was the conductor wearing a turban?
   Yes / No

10. Was someone playing the flute?
    Yes / No

11. Was someone clapping?
    Yes / No

12. Was there a child present?
    Yes / No

13. Was anyone wearing a tuxedo?
    Yes / No

14. What famous Disney character was on the poster?
    a. Tinker Bell
    b. Mickey
    c. Goofy
    d. There were no Disney celebrities on that billboard.

15. Which group was featured?
    a. The Lora Hoot Singers
    b. Wolfy and the Little Pigs
    c. The Cool Jazz Daddies
    d. The Bee Bopping Babes

16. Which instruments were missing from the band that you saw playing on the billboard?

    a. A piano   b. A harp

    c. A violin   d. A tuba

    e. None was missing. f. All were missing.

17. What was at the very top of the billboard?

    a. A star

    b. The name of the show

    c. The conductor

    d. A face with a wide open mouth

18. Were there any celestial objects in that picture?

    a. Yes, planets

    b. Yes, stars and a moon

    c. Yes, stars

    d. Nope, no celestial objects here

Monsters, Inc. Mike and Sulley to the Rescue!

? **Pop Quiz!** There's a monstrous lot of doors in front of you. Take a quick look and then join the queue.

1. There was a huge green monster mouth holding something. What was it holding?

    a. A pink door with flowers on it

    b. A Monstropolis cab with the doors hanging open

    c. A white circle with a huge M in it and an eye

    d. Children's toys stamped "Hazardous to monsters. Stay back."

2. There were a lot of monsters moving through the doors. Were any of them wearing glasses?
Yes / No

3. Were any of the monsters dripping with green slime?
Yes / No

4. Were any of the monsters wearing hats?
Yes / No

End of Pop Quiz

Outside Queue

5. What prestigious award(s) did *Monster News* win?
   a. They were a third-time winner of the "Monstrosity" for most annoying news on the air.
   b. They won best new exposé for their piece "Now Would be a Good Time to Panic," exposing the dangers posed by human children.
   c. They were awarded best news program for monsters endowed with more than three eyes based on their multi-image presentation style.
   d. They won 13 Screamy Awards; there was a trophy and everything.

6. *Monster News* was awarded a trophy for accomplishments in TV journalism. What important body part was missing from that trophy?
   a. The head
   b. The arms
   c. The whole body was missing, it was just an eye.
   d. Monsters don't like trophies.

7. There is a poster for Monsters Inc. What appears in this poster four times?
   a. The Monsters Inc. symbol of a circle with an M and an eye
   b. Clocks
   c. Hard hats
   d. Monsters sporting just one eye

8. There is a poster for a restaurant you could visit in Monstropolis called Harryhausen's (if you weren't so human that is). What kind of food does it sell?
   a. Tacos
   b. Hamburgers
   c. Sushi
   d. I don't know. The chef is a monster. He probably serves eyeballs and worms in a lovely mud sauce.

9. There is a picture of Harryhausen's chef. What kind of monster is he?
   a. Octopus shaped
   b. Hairy all over
   c. Multi-eyed
   d. Slimy

10. If you see a human child on the loose in Monstropolis, what should you do?
   a. Turn off the lights and hide under the bed until it goes away.
   b. Panic.
   c. Contact the CDA right away.
   d. Call *Monster News*. They will want to interview you. You are going to be on TV!

11. What does CDA stand for?
   a. Child Detection Agency
   b. Child Deception Association
   c. Child Detriment Alliance
   d. Child Detention Authority

12. How many eyes do the monsters working for the CDA have?

    a. 1

    b. 2

    c. 7

    d. Well that anyone's guess.

13. What is the significance of the number "415"?

    a. It is the number of tentacles believed to be possessed by Harryhausen's chef.

    b. It is the number on one of the CDA workers.

    c. It is the area code for Monstropolis.

    d. It is the number on the Monstropolis taxi that's parked by the queue.

14. You are about to enter the MTA. What is that?

    a. The Monstropolis Transit Authority

    b. The Monsters Training Area

    c. The Monstrous Towering Apartments

    d. I'm not sure, but I think it is not advisable for humans to enter.

15. There is a sign telling you what you will find inside the MTA. What's inside?

    a. Monsters learning to be more skilled scarers

    b. Tickets and schedules

    c. Apartments for super-sized monsters

    d. The unknown

16. There is a framed picture of downtown Monstropolis. What's in it?

    a. Cars

    b. Trees

    c. Large buildings

    d. All of the above

    e. None of the above

Entering the MTA

17. In the window of the scheduling booth there is another poster for Monstropolis. It features some monsters out for a drive. What unfortunate thing is happening to them?

   a. They are about to be stepped on by a larger monster.
   b. They are becoming lunch for another monster.
   c. They have a human child aboard and don't yet know it.
   d. They are about to drive off a cliff.

18. There is a sign in the window of the transit authority to "All Monster Passengers." What does it tell them?

   a. If you have multiple heads on one body, you are only required to pay for one ticket.
   b. If you belch fire, you are not allowed to sit directly behind the driver.
   c. Body slime drippers and oozers are required to clean the seat after use as a courtesy to the next passenger.
   d. All of the above
   e. All but 'c'

19. What is the symbol of the Monstropolis cab company?

   a. The word "cab" inside a big mouth with fangs
   b. A big wheel with an eye in the center
   c. A monster cab with one big eye looking out the window
   d. A yellow cab with feet instead of wheels

20. There is another poster for Monsters Inc. Check its inhabitants. Do any of them have fur?

   Yes / No

21. Which delicious foods can you get at Harryhausen's?
    a. Swill and Sour Soup
    b. Glop Stickers
    c. Caterpillar Roll
    d. Both 'a' and 'b'
    e. Both 'a' and 'c'

22. You will find a public phone. Check the phonebook provided. Which of the following is not listed?
    a. Monsters, Inc.
    b. Screamtronics
    c. Cyclops Optical
    d. Tony's Grossery

Video Screen Quiz
Search for the answers to questions 23 to 27 on the video screen.

23. What would the Monstropolis Chamber of Commerce like to welcome you with?
    a. A Monstropolis cheer: Go, go, go on home!
    b. A bouquet of mushrooms
    c. Big hairy arms
    d. A visit to the CDA if we find you

24. What is Scarodynamics?
    a. The scientific process used to condition and train flying monsters
    b. The process used to match each human child to its ideal monster
    c. The physical process that occurs in humans when proper fear has been fostered
    d. The uglification process used to create the gleaming city we call Monstropolis

25. Whose family founded Monsters, Inc.
    a. Henry J. Waternoose's
    b. James P. Sullivan's
    c. Randall Boggs's
    d. Mike Wazowski's

26. What does a test of the Child Detection
Emergency Broadcast System look like on the
screen?
    a. You see and hear the words, "Only you can
       prevent child infestation."
    b. You see downtown Monstropolis with
       screaming monsters running in circles on
       the streets.
    c. There's a large picture of a human child
       and the words "It Is Time To Panic."
    d. You see a circle with a screaming monster
       inside it.

27. Monstropolis Transit Authority provides
some useful travel information. What is it?
    a. Humans are not allowed on Monstropolis
       trains, buses, and cabs.
    b. Buses and trains leave hourly.
       Monstropolis city cabs are available any
       time.
    c. Monstropolis trains are reserved for
       passengers who fit inside the vehicle.
    d. Buses and trains are available to riders
       regardless of size as long as they don't
       squish the vehicle.

Note: This concludes the questions from the video.

28. Who is the Scarer of the Month according
to a huge sign?
    a. Mike Wazowski
    b. James P. Sullivan
    c. Randall Boggs
    d. Boo (She scared all of Monstropolis.)

29. Treasure Hunt Time! See how many of these monster supplies you can find before you get scared away.

- ❏ A helicopter
- ❏ A behemoth
- ❏ A thumbs-up
- ❏ A suggestion on how to conserve scream
- ❏ Golden eyelashes
- ❏ A "Bag O Calories"
- ❏ "Blort"
- ❏ Something that is taste free
- ❏ An eyeball
- ❏ "Single Len 2-D Special"
- ❏ A Monsterious newspaper
- ❏ The proud parents
- ❏ The Really Big 'N' Tall Shop

MuppetVision 3D

1. There is a big sign for MuppetVision 3D as you enter the line. Something on the sign has been knocked askew. What is it?
   a. A gussied-up pig is about to fall off.
   b. The "3D" is loose.
   c. All of the stars are coming loose.
   d. The whole sign is about to fall.

2. A large yellow arrow directs you to the entrance. What is the arrow painted on?
   a. A big blue garage door
   b. A large wall
   c. A chicken's belly
   d. The roof

Spaceship

3. Off to the side, you will see a parked spaceship. It is very unusual looking with many interesting adornments. One of the features provides a hint about what type of Muppet might operate this spaceship. What is it?

    a. The ship has a huge set of whiskers. I think it is run by rat Muppets.

    b. Webbed feet, lots of them. It must be operated by froctopuses.

    c. It has large silver wings. The Muppets aboard must be birds.

    d. A cute springy tail. This ship is manned by pigs; I didn't know swine flew.

4. What will the Muppets use to blast off?

    a. The bike pedals sticking out the bottom

    b. A giant slingshot just off to the side

    c. Four separate blasters on the ends of long arms

    d. A large magnet on the front will pull them into space.

Muppet Contraption

5. Treasure Hunt Time! You've come to a Muppet named Beaker, who is strapped to a chair. He is surrounded by an invention. See how many of these inventive treasures you can find before that machine does something scary to poor Beaker.

- ❑ A plunger
- ❑ Some purple goop
- ❑ Bellows
- ❑ A rubber ducky
- ❑ A bike chain
- ❑ Three camera lenses
- ❑ Three roller skates
- ❑ A spinning wheel in red and yellow
- ❑ A knee pad

- ❏ A way to make a lot of wind
- ❏ Three different gloves
- ❏ A crank
- ❏ A place for Kermit
- ❏ A 10-pound weight
- ❏ Three springs
- ❏ A crutch
- ❏ A face in an unusual place
- ❏ Three fingernails
- ❏ Muppet 3D FX Labs
- ❏ A considerable underbite
- ❏ A way to be much louder

6. Something is just busting to open up. What is it?

    a. The 3D film vault

    b. The zipper on a rather rotund Muppet

    c. The curtains covering a window

    d. The top of a crate marked "Stuffing and Stuff"

7. This mysterious busting-open thing, what does it feature that you wouldn't expect?

    a. A zipper   b. Hands

    c. Padlocks   d. Eyes

8. There is a movie poster for *Breakfast, Lunch and Dinner at Tiffany's* featuring Miss Piggy. Which of the following delicacies is not on Miss Piggy's plate?

    a. Caramel popcorn   b. Pancakes

    c. Chocolate syrup   d. Chinese takeout

    e. They are all on her plate.

9. You will see a door for Muppet 3D FX Lab. What is unusual about this door?

    a. It is upside down.

    b. The doorknob has eyes.

    c. It will never open.

    d. You can't close it.

10. You will come to a movie poster for *The Dogfather*. Which of the following is true about it?

    a. The Dogfather is holding a cat.

    b. The marionette handle is made from a beloved treat.

    c. The Dogfather is using a banana for a gun.

    d. All of the above

    e. All but 'c'

Disaster Effects

11. There is a storage area for "Disaster Effects" next to a dining area. What do they promise to do?

    a. "We'll blow your movie sky high."

    b. "We'll make your movie a total disaster."

    c. "We'll destroy your movie."

    d. "We'll add real excitement to your movie."

12. Whose stuff is marked "do not open"?

    a. Miss Piggy's: Keep out, all mine.

    b. Muppet 3D FX Lab's

    c. Pandora's

    d. Sweetums's

13. What kind of disaster has a spigot on its container?

    a. Sinkholes   b. Tidal waves

    c. Rotten eggs   d. Floods

14. What kind of disaster involves clothing?

    a. Disco attire   b. Wedgies

    c. Plumber's pants   d. Smelly socks

15. What type of disaster requires some assembly?

    a. An icy road

    b. A volcanic explosion

    c. An angry mob

    d. A banana-peel event

16. Someone appears to have created a disaster all his own. Gonzo The Great has missed his target and gone through the wall on his motorcycle. What happened?
- a. The target has feet. It ran away when it saw Gonzo coming.
- b. Gonzo was blindfolded and couldn't see where he was going.
- c. Gonzo was trying to hit the target while riding backwards. Bad idea.
- d. Gonzo's aim was just way off.

17. There is a poster for MuppetVision 3D that makes some promises. What is not promised?
- a. "Coming Soon! MuppetVision 4D"
- b. "So Real You'll Think You're There"
- c. "Now even better in DOLBY 3D!"
- d. They are all promised.

Security Station

18. Soon you will arrive at the security station. In case of emergency, what should you do to reach security?
- a. Try to break in.
- b. Sound the gong.
- c. Cluck like a chicken.
- d. Shout "Hey, free donuts!"

19. Treasure Hunt! See how many of these security company possessions you can find before they come to arrest you for loitering.
- ❑ The name of the security company
- ❑ A small toy car
- ❑ Two bananas
- ❑ A ham on a motorcycle
- ❑ A PBJ sandwich
- ❑ Chopsticks
- ❑ The location of the key
- ❑ A donut

- ❑ Someone wanted for impersonating a comic
- ❑ A delivery sticker for K Frog
- ❑ A pink coffee mug
- ❑ A telephone
- ❑ A black fan
- ❑ A request for a jet engine to be added to a computer

The Hall

20. What must you be to enter the theater?
    a. A Muppet
    b. Shorter than the arch
    c. A little bit crazy
    d. Approved by Miss Piggy

21. Find a part of the building that is not what it appears. What is it?
    a. It is a door, or is it?
    b. It is a ceiling, at least it should be.
    c. It is a wall, or maybe not?
    d. It is a window, at least I think it is. I guess I will never know.

22. There are two old men who have come prepared to let the Muppets know what they think of the show. What will they use?
    a. Blindfolds and ear muffs
    b. Signs with "boo" in big red letters
    c. Tomatoes
    d. Surely old gentlemen would never resort to such inappropriate behavior.

23. Muppet 3D FX Labs has some rather unexpected departments you will pass on your way in. Which of the following is not a department of Muppet 3D FX Labs?
   a. The department of making things appear closer in your rearview mirror
   b. The department of making things more expensive then we can afford
   c. The stress testing department
   d. The department of crying wolf

24. Someone is, shall we say, wearing a musical instrument. What instrument is it?
   a. An accordion
   b. A tuba
   c. A drum
   d. A bird whistle

25. Find a picture of Kermit. He is sporting some high fashion. What is he wearing?
   a. A tuxedo and top hat for the Ritz effect
   b. A leather coat and jeans for that just-too-cool look
   c. An Hawaiian shirt and shorts for a tropical vibe
   d. Lots of bling for that rich frog thing

26. The Muppet cast has autographed a poster. Which Muppet uses a star in his or her autograph?
   a. The Great Gonzo
   b. Miss Piggy
   c. Fozzie Bear
   d. Kermit the Frog

27. Whose autograph is ripped?
   a. Kermit the Frog
   b. The Great Gonzo
   c. Ralph
   d. Animal

The Prop Room

28. Treasure Hunt Time! You have entered the prop storage area. It is packed full of Muppet treasure. See how many props you can find before curtain time.

- ❑ A fake Mickey Mouse
- ❑ Indian bedspreads
- ❑ A violin in its case
- ❑ Two lava lamps
- ❑ A Statue of Liberty hat
- ❑ A collection of pinwheels
- ❑ A bomb
- ❑ A penguin's lunch
- ❑ A brick wall
- ❑ One maraca
- ❑ Tinkertoys
- ❑ A movie camera
- ❑ A reluctant orchestra
- ❑ A blue crayon
- ❑ One banjo
- ❑ A basketball
- ❑ A flowerpot hat doing a jig
- ❑ A telescope
- ❑ A bent nail
- ❑ A torch
- ❑ Two pineapples
- ❑ A red tutu
- ❑ A tripod
- ❑ TNT
- ❑ A tiger
- ❑ A birdcage containing something rather fishy
- ❑ A hatbox
- ❑ Something that is highly magnified
- ❑ Famous art featuring Muppets
- ❑ A unicycle
- ❑ A feathered boa
- ❑ Miss Piggy's luggage

- ☐ Something to "Open in the event of an event."
- ☐ Horse No. 5
- ☐ A bird's nest with three eggs about to fly away
- ☐ King Tut
- ☐ A fishing net
- ☐ Scientific Doohickey Company
- ☐ A boxing glove
- ☐ Banana puree
- ☐ A small cannon
- ☐ A putter
- ☐ An industrial-sized jack
- ☐ Snowshoes
- ☐ Patriotic paraphernalia
- ☐ A fire hydrant

The Twilight Zone Tower of Terror™

Collection Time! Note: For this ride you have a special Collection to work on. Look for the initials "HTH." You will find them all around you. Earn 1 point for each "HTH" you locate.

Outside the Hollywood Tower Hotel

1. What is the name of the hotel you are about to check into? **FP**

    a. The Tower of Terror
    b. The Hollywood Tower of Terror Hotel
    c. The Hollywood Tower Hotel
    d. The Hotel at the End of the Universe

2. Were all of the letters present on the Hotel's sign? **FP**

Yes / No

3. It looks like something terrible has happened to this hotel. Perhaps you should rethink checking in. What do you guess caused all the damage?

a. Lightning; I can see the lightning marks.

b. A bad earthquake; Hollywood is in California after all.

c. It appears that the vines were allowed to grow all over the hotel and have damaged its structure. They need a gardener!

d. It is in "The Twilight Zone"; that is disaster enough for any hotel.

e. Both 'a' and 'c'

f. Both 'b' and 'c'

4. Does the hotel have any gargoyles?

Yes / No

5. Does the hotel have any pipes visible on the outside?

Yes / No

6. Do you get a view of the hotel pool?

Yes / No

7. Does the garden feature a fountain?

Yes / No

The Lobby

8. You have entered the hotel lobby. As there are a lot of guests waiting to check in, you may as well have a look around. Find a small table where two people have been playing a game. What were they playing?

a. Backgammon   b. Tarot cards

c. Monopoly   d. Cards

9. Did they have an ashtray?
   Yes / No

10. Which of the following was not on this table?
   a. A ring on the wood made by a cup
   b. A pitcher
   c. A lamp shaped like a lady
   d. A book

11. It appears to have been a while since Maid Service and Maintenance have attended to the lobby. What indicators suggest management needs to hire new help?
   a. Cobwebs   b. Dead plants
   c. Dust   d. Crumbled wall
   e. All of the above f. All but 'd'

12. Treasure Hunt Time! Look around the lobby. See how many of these dusty treasures you can find before they disappear into "The Twilight Zone."
   ❑   An Asian planter
   ❑   Brick
   ❑   A tapestry
   ❑   Gold tassels
   ❑   Lace
   ❑   A vase with dead flowers
   ❑   A very long dragon
   ❑   A long curly tongue with a job
   ❑   Used napkins
   ❑   Five spoons all in a row
   ❑   A teapot
   ❑   Four wheels
   ❑   A dusty bird of the night
   ❑   A pipe
   ❑   A child's doll
   ❑   A briefcase
   ❑   An umbrella
   ❑   The number "1102"

13. You will come to a directory. Where would you expect to find the Steam Bath?
     a. The lobby level
     b. The lower level
     c. The mezzanine
     d. The penthouse level

14. Some of the letters on the Elevator directory have disappeared. What letters are now in "The Twilight Zone"?
     a. A C U W R V   b. A B O O R E
     c. A B U O W V   d. M I C K E Y

15. You will come to a clock featuring a mighty battle. Who is fighting?
     a. An eagle and a snake
     b. A dragon and a knight
     c. A lion and a unicorn
     d. A sorcerer and his apprentice

16. There are some things missing from this clock that might make it more useful. What are they?
     a. The numbers 1, 2, 3, 6, and 7
     b. Part of one of the hands
     c. Both of the above
     d. Nothing is missing, but I am late.

17. What is important about the number "22"?
     a. It is the number of the top floor in this hotel.
     b. It is the number of a room that's still available.
     c. It is only important to those trying to count more than 21 things.
     d. It is on a rather big and impressive wooden door.

18. There is a beautiful picture of a lady. She seems to be royalty. How many crowns can be found in this picture? **FP**
   a. 1-She is wearing it.
   b. 2-Every girl needs a spare.
   c. 3-She is in a shop and is choosing.
   d. 4-You can never have too much bling.

19. If you check out the luggage, you may discover that someone with the initials G.K. planned on some fun during his stay. What was G.K. hoping to do?
   a. Play golf
   b. Go to the theater
   c. Swim in the pool
   d. I don't know; he probably wanted to do all that stuff.

20. The hotel gift shop has a display of presents that they recommend for mother. What two gifts do they suggest?
   a. A diary with a silver lock and a pearl necklace
   b. A jeweled picture frame and an intricate looking pen
   c. A large flowered vase and a gold thimble
   d. A stuffed Mickey Mouse and a T-shirt

21. Which of the following is not on the desk?
   a. A box with drawers
   b. A desk lamp featuring a camel
   c. Some mahjong tiles
   d. A magnifying glass
   e. All of the above
   f. All except 'b'

? **Library Pop Quiz!** Once you arrive in the library, direct your attention to the TV screen. You will be shown a brief story of "The Twilight Zone." When it is over you will undoubtedly be shown to your room to relax. When you've departed the library, see how much you remember from the TV clip.

22. What do you need to unlock the door? **FP**
    a. The key of imagination
    b. The key of fantasy
    c. The key of fear
    d. The key with the right room number

23. What is beyond the door? **FP**
    a. An imaginary dimension
    b. The fourth dimension
    c. The lost dimension
    d. Another dimension

24. What are the three things you are told about the dimension beyond the door? **FP**
    a. That it is a dimension of sight, smell, and mind
    b. That it is a dimension of sound, sight, and mind
    c. That it is a dimension of sound, sight, and thought
    d. That it is a dimension of senses, feeling, and thought

25. Something made of glass is broken. What is it? **FP**
    a. A mirror. There's seven years' bad luck!
    b. A window. Do they have homeowner's insurance in this dimension?
    c. A wine glass. I hope it wasn't red wine. It can be murder to get out of the carpet.
    d. A chandelier, but I saw no phantom.

26. Which of these things were not seen in the introduction on the TV screen? *FP*
   a. A phone
   b. E=mc^2
   c. An eyeball
   d. A clock
   e. I saw all of the above.

27. What year is it? *FP*
   a. 1910
   b. 1926
   c. 1939
   d. 1953

28. Who likes to come to the Hollywood Tower Hotel? *FP*
   a. The show business elite
   b. The very rich
   c. Vacationing families on a budget
   d. Anyone really; the rates are fantastic.

29. Who got onto the elevator? Check all who got aboard. *FP*
   a. A fabulously dressed couple, probably movie stars
   b. A bellhop
   c. A set of twins
   d. A little boy
   e. A little girl
   f. An older woman who might be the nanny
   g. A pet dog
   h. An old gentleman

30. Was the child carrying a toy? *FP*
   Yes / No

31. What disaster occurred at the Hollywood Tower Hotel on that fateful night? *FP*
   a. Lightning struck.
   b. An earthquake hit.
   c. A volcano surfaced just underneath the elevator shaft.
   d. All of the above. It was a very bad time to be staying in that hotel.

32. When disaster struck what happened? **FP**
    a. The building was covered in lightning.
    b. The guests lit up like a Christmas tree.
    c. The elevator plummeted.
    d. Part of the hotel's front disappeared.
    e. All of the above.

33. What is still in operation waiting for you?
FP
    a. A guest elevator
    b. A service elevator
    c. An escalator
    d. The stairs; I think I could use some
       exercise.

34. Where does this elevator travel? **FP**
    a. To the basement
    b. To the very top of the building
    c. To your room, of course
    d. Directly to "The Twilight Zone"

End of Pop Quiz

The Boiler Room
35. Treasure Hunt Time! Look around the boiler room for these strange, discarded, and just plain dirty items before you step onto the elevator.

If you are in the Standby line, search for these treasures:
- ❑ Spilled paint
- ❑ A crank
- ❑ A striped chair
- ❑ At least 20 gauges
- ❑ A black barrel with a white lid
- ❑ The word "Danger" in red
- ❑ A "Safety Check"
- ❑ Three mops
- ❑ A bell

- ❏ A stool
- ❏ An old chest of drawers
- ❏ A small electrical box with red and black buttons and a light
- ❏ A surprise in "1105"
- ❏ A fan
- ❏ A tin can with no label, filled with bolts
- ❏ A thermometer
- ❏ A hook
- ❏ A ladder
- ❏ A furnace
- ❏ A lunchbox
- ❏ Frayed rope
- ❏ A hammer

If you are in the FASTPASS line, search for these items in the boiler room. You won't be able to see the treasures visible from the Standby queue. **FP**

- ❏ A pair of glasses
- ❏ A child wearing a white dress
- ❏ A ring of old keys
- ❏ A yellow wheel
- ❏ An ominous warning
- ❏ A harmonica
- ❏ A moving arrow
- ❏ A chain
- ❏ A red rag
- ❏ At least 20 gauges

36. You are just about to board your service elevator. How many floors are there? **FP**
   a. None b. 11
   c. 12 d. 13

Now it is time to secure all of your possessions and prepare to enter…"The Twilight Zone." Cue ominous music here.

Hollywood Land Answers

Disney Animation: Turtle Talk with Crush waiting area
1) Total Treasures found _____
2) Number of items collected _____

Disney Junior—Live On Stage!
1) c. Elephants
2) a. They are sitting on top of tall poles.
3) d. A lion
4) Total Treasures found _____
5) Number of colors found _____
6) Dance points earned _____

Hyperion Theater Pop Quizzes:
Moon Over Monrovia Billboard
1) b. Donald and Daisy
2) a. The Moon
3) d. Ducky
4) c. Making music
5) c. 2
6) d. 4
7) a. Elephants
8) b. Nothing
9) a. A skyscraper
10) c. Yes, she had on a bracelet.
11) b. A bow and a top hat
12) Yes
Down Catalina Way Billboard
1) a. Mickey and Minnie
2) d. Green grapes
3) c. 5
4) b. Pink
5) a. A flying fish
6) c. Dancing
7) d. A vest
8) a. A fluffy skirt and a tube top

9) c. Stars
10) a. Orange
11) d. 4
12) d. No birds there.
13) b. Yes, searchlights
14) c. 7
15) Yes

Hollywood Pictures Cinetone News Billboard

1) c. 2
2) a. A backward hat
3) d. Goofy
4) No
5) Yes
6) Yes
7) No
8) Yes
9) Yes
10) No
11) a. 2
12) b. News
13) Yes

On the Great Stage Billboard

1) Yes
2) No
3) Yes
4) Yes
5) No
6) Yes
7) Yes
8) No
9) Yes
10) No
11) No
12) No
13) Yes
14) d. There were no Disney celebrities on that billboard.
15) a. The Lora Hoot Singers
16) b. A harp
17) d. A face with a wide open mouth
18) c. Yes, stars

Monsters, Inc. Mike and Sulley to the Rescue!
Pop Quiz (Answers 1 to 4)
1) c. A white circle with a huge M in it and an eye
2) Yes
3) No
4) Yes

Outside Queue
5) d. They won 13 Screamy Awards.
6) a. The head
7) b. Clocks
8) c. Sushi
9) a. Octopus shaped
10) c. Contact the CDA right away.
11) a. Child Detection Agency
12) d. Well that's anyone's guess.
13) d. It is the number on the Monstropolis taxi that's parked by the queue.
14) a. The Monstropolis Transit Authority
15) b. Tickets and schedules
16) d. All of the above

Entering the MTA
17) b. They are becoming lunch for another monster.
18) d. All of the above
19) c. A monster cab with one big eye looking out the window
20) Yes
21) e. Both 'a' and 'c'
22) a. Monsters, Inc.

Video Screen Quiz (Answers 23 to 27)
23) c. Big hairy arms
24) b. The process used to match each human child to its ideal monster.
25) a. Henry J. Waternoose's
26) d. You see a circle with a screaming monster inside it.
27) b. Buses and trains leave hourly. Monstropolis city cabs are available any time.
28) c. Randall Boggs
29) Total Treasures found _____

MuppetVision 3D

1) b. The "3D" is loose.
2) a. A big blue garage door

Spaceship

3) d. A cute springy tail. This ship is manned by pigs.
4) c. Four separate blasters on the ends of long arms

Muppet Contraption

5) Total Treasures found _____
6) a. The 3D film vault
7) d. Eyes
8) a. Caramel popcorn
9) c. It will never open.
10) e. All but 'c'

Disaster Effects

11) b. "We'll make your movie a total disaster."
12) c. Pandora's
13) a. Sinkholes
14) d. Smelly socks
15) c. An angry mob
16) d. Gonzo's aim was just way off.
17) a. "Coming Soon! MuppetVision 4D"

Security Station

18) d. Shout "Hey, free donuts!"
19) Total Treasures found _____

The Hunt

20) b. Shorter than the arch
21) a. It is a door, or is it?
22) c. Tomatoes
23) d. The department of crying wolf
24) c. A drum
25) b. A leather coat and jeans for that just-too-cool look
26) a. The Great Gonzo
27) d. Animal

The Prop Room

28) Total Props found _____

The Twilight Zone Tower of Terror™

1) c. The Hollywood Tower Hotel
2) No
3) a. Lightning; I can see the lightning marks.
4) No

The Twilight Zone Tower of Terror. cont'd.

5) *Yes*

6) *No*

7) *Yes*

The Lobby

8) *d. Cards*

9) *Yes*

10) *b. A pitcher*

11) *e. All of the above*

12) *Total Lobby Treasures found* _____

13) *b. The lower level*

14) *c. A B U O W V*

15) *a. An eagle and a snake*

16) *c. Both of the above*

17) *d. It is on a rather big and impressive wooden door.*

18) *b. 2-Every girl needs a spare.*

19) *a. Play golf*

20) *c. A large flowered vase and a gold thimble*

21) *e. All of the above*

Library Pop Quiz (Answers 22 to 34)

22) *a. The key of imagination*

23) *d. Another dimension*

24) *b. That it is a dimension of sound, sight, and mind.*

25) *b. A window*

26) *a. A phone*

27) *c. 1939*

28) *a. The show business elite*

29) *a. A fabulously dressed couple, b. A bellhop, e. A little girl, f. An older woman who might be the nanny*

30) *Yes*

31) *a. Lightning struck.*

32) *e. All of the above.*

33) *b. A service elevator*

34) *d. Directly to "The Twilight Zone"*

Boiler Room

35) *Total Boiler Room Treasures found* _____

36) *d. 13*

Special Collection

Total "HRH" initials collected _____

Paradise Pier

California Screamin' Billboard Memory Games

? Pop Quizzes!

Before you get into *either* the long Standby queue for California Screamin' *or* its FASTPASS queue, walk quickly over to the giant old-fashioned billboards that line the wall of the Boardwalk area just prior to the ride.

You will see four of them. Take a long look at them, because we are going to play memory games. To have a chance, you will need to give the billboards a hard look. You may choose to examine as many of them as you want. There are pop quizzes for all four.

Billboard No. 1: for Coca-Cola

1. What did the Coca-Cola billboard say?
   a. Chill out with a bottle of Coca-Cola
   b. Paradise in a bottle
   c. Ice cold and refreshing
   d. Delicious and Refreshing

2. It seemed to be a sunny day at the beach, perfect. Did everyone have a hat?

Yes / No

3. There was a little girl out for a walk. Who was with her?

a. Her dad

b. Her mom

c. Her two brothers

d. No one, someone find a policeman, we have a lost kid there.

4. There was a man selling Coke from a cart on the boardwalk. What was on top of his cart?

a. Several bottles of Coke

b. An silver ice bucket with Coke bottles sticking out

c. Three bottles of Coke and a cash register

d. He had nothing on the cart but he was holding a bottle of Coke out to a customer.

5. Did any of the people have a dog on a leash?

Yes / No

6. Had the Coke salesman managed to sell a bottle to anyone?

a. Yes, a man

b. Yes, a lady

c. Yes, a child

d. No, he needs to step it up.

7. What was the child wearing to the beach today?

a. An old-fashioned bathing suit in baby blue with a matching ruffled hat

b. A white blouse and a black striped skirt with gloves

c. A white dress, hat, socks, and buckle shoes – a little overdressed for the beach if you ask me.

   d. A white cover-up robe that went most of
      the way to the floor with striped socks and
      black shoes.

8. The child was holding a doll.
   True or False?

9. There was a couple on the far right side of
the picture. The lady appeared to be offering
something to the man. What?
   a. Her hand, how romantic!
   b. A bottle of Coke naturally
   c. A kiss. Oh my, shocking!
   d. Her back; they seemed to be having a
      disagreement. Someone needs to chill out
      with a bottle of Coke.

10. The people at the beach seemed to be
dressed very formally. Could you see anyone's
legs on the beach itself?
   Yes / No

11. Could you see the sun in the sky?
   Yes / No

12 Were there seagulls flying around?
   a. Yes, and that accounts for all the
      umbrellas.
   b. No, there were no food stands, so no
      seagulls either.

13. How was the little girl's hair fixed?
   a. It was long and light brown with a bow.
   b. It was in two long blond braids.
   c. It was in a short blond bob.
   d. The child had a bonnet on; I could not see
      her hair.

14. How many bottles of Cola were visible in the billboard?

a. 5   b. 6

c. 7   d. 8

Billboard No. 2: for Garden Dining

1. What a lovely place to dine. What was its name?

a. Paradise Garden Grill

b. Mickey's Steakhouse

c. Boardwalk Pizza and Pasta

d. Beach Club Dining

e. All of the above restaurants were listed.

f. Only 'a' and 'c'

2. Was it sunny out?

Yes / No

3. The waitress was coming. What was she bringing?

a. A burger and fries

b. Looked like a mug of beer

c. Several glasses of tea and a plate of pasta

d. The menu

4. What was the waitress wearing?

a. A blue blouse, a blue skirt thigh length, and a half apron. Oh, and a hat naturally.

b. A black floor-length dress and a full white apron. She had her hair in a bun.

c. A red-and-white striped dress and a fluffy white apron. Her hair was up in a white bonnet.

d. Long black pants and a white blouse with her hair in a tightly pulled back braid.

5. Did all the diners in view appear to have a drink?

Yes / No

6. Was someone cleaning up a spill?
   Yes / No

7. The lady in the foreground of the picture was wearing a very conspicuous piece of jewelry today. What was it?
   a. A necklace
   b. A bracelet
   c. A cameo
   d. A diamond ring! So that's why that man was on one knee. I thought he'd dropped his napkin.

8. Were all of the diners adults?
   a. No, there was a boy, too.
   b. No, there was a girl, too.
   c. No, there was also a baby. Up too late if you ask me.
   d. Yes, there were only adults.

9. Was a fountain in the center of the garden?
   Yes / No

10. Was the garden decorated with lights?
    Yes / No

11. Was there a view of the beach?
    Yes / No

12. There were large blue circles in the top right and left of the billboard. What was written in the one on the left?
    a. Award-winning Clam Chowder
    b. Dancing at 8PM
    c. Formal Dress Required
    d. Live Music

13. What was written in the circle on the right?
   a. Beach Front Dining
   b. By the Bay
   c. Dining Alfresco
   d. Sunday Brunch at 11 AM

Billboard No. 3: for Soar

1. What did the poster tell you to do?
   a. Soar by the sea.
   b. Soar at Paradise Pier.
   c. Soar at the shore.
   d. Soar over California.

2. The poster featured two rides you might try out today. What were they?
   a. Mickey's Fun Wheel and Golden Zephyr
   b. Golden Zephyr and Silly Symphony Swings
   c. Silly Symphony Swings and King Triton's Carousel
   d. Jumpin' Jellyfish and Mickey's Fun Wheel
   e. Both 'a' and 'd'

3. In the billboard, could you see the ground?
   Yes / No

4. Were there any live animals?
   Yes / No

5. There was a lot of wind on these rides. Something was flying away. What was it?
   a. A bird   b. A hat
   c. A balloon   d. A bird
   e. All of the above   f. Only 'b' and 'c'

6. Did you see any plants?
   Yes / No

7. Someone had a stick. What was it being used for?
   a. Conducting
   b. Poking
   c. It was a walking stick.
   d. A boy was using it to knock off a girl's hat.

8. The children were having fun flying in the Golden Zephyr. Describe its wings.
   a. They were striped red and white.
   b. They were plain silver. A bit off for a golden zephyr, if you ask me.
   c. They were striped with red and featured a star in a circle.
   d. What wings?

9. Mickey Mouse was present in this billboard. What was he doing?
   a. Signing autographs
   b. Riding in the Golden Zephyr
   c. Conducting
   d. I think you are pulling my leg; that was a kid wearing mouse ears.

10. The words Paradise Pier were visible in the billboard.
    True or False?

11. The children in the billboard were dressed in modern-day clothing.
    True or False?

12. Donald Duck was also visible in the Soar billboard. What was he doing?
    a. Signing autographs
    b. Riding on the Golden Zephyr
    c. Flying
    d. Now I know you are pulling my leg; Donald wasn't there.

Billboard No. 4: for Paradise Pier

1. The two main figures in the billboard were a man and a woman. What were they doing?
   a. Walking along the shore in the shallow waves
   b. Sitting at a cafe table sipping drinks and gazing at the water
   c. Sitting on the sand holding hands
   d. Standing on a balcony looking out at the ocean

2. What was the lady wearing?
   a. A green one-piece bathing suit and a bow
   b. An old-fashioned purple dress
   c. A flowing white beach dress
   d. An itsy bitsy teeny weenie yellow polka dot bikini

3. What was the man wearing?
   a. An old-fashioned man's swimsuit
   b. A green striped suit with a tie
   c. Baggy pants and a white linen shirt
   d. A surfer Speedo in neon green

4. Were they wearing hats?
   Yes / No

5. Did they have a pet with them?
   a. Yes, a dog on a leash
   b. Yes, a monkey on the woman's shoulder
   c. Yes, a bird perched next to them
   d. No, there were no pets.

6. Were there any children in this picture?
   Yes / No

7. What was visible in the sky other than the clouds?
   a. An airplane
   b. Hang gliders
   c. Sea gulls
   d. An alien spaceship

8. Many people sitting on the beach had something with them. What?
   a. Umbrellas
   b. Beach balls
   c. Beach blankets
   d. Bottles of Coca-Cola

9. Were there any boats in the water?
   Yes / No

10. Was anyone swimming in the ocean?
    Yes / No

11. Did the beach offer any shade?
    a. Yes, inside a restaurant
    b. Yes, under a large tree
    c. Yes, in and under a three-story shelter
    d. No, there was no shade.

12. What was the motto for Paradise Pier on the billboard?
    a. Come Be a Kid Again
    b. At the Rainbow's End
    c. A Mix of Heaven and Earth
    d. Between Sea and Sky

13. Could you actually see Paradise Pier on the billboard?
    a. Of course. It was the roller coaster, right?
    b. Nope. Now that's pretty weird.

Golden Zephyr

The Golden Zephyr was original to Disney California Adventure. It opened with the park in 2001.

1. Is this ride older or younger than you?

2. Is this ride older or younger than your Dad?

3. Treasure Hunt Time! See if you can find these treasures in the park area around you as you wait for blastoff.
- ❑ Blue umbrellas
- ❑ Golden waves
- ❑ A life preserver float
- ❑ A mermaid
- ❑ A three-story window
- ❑ A gazebo
- ❑ Long strings of lights
- ❑ A blue door
- ❑ A long red pipe
- ❑ The number 1
- ❑ At least two suns
- ❑ Mickey Mouse

4. How do you, the rocket operator, make your ship go up?
- a. I pull up on the control stick.
- b. I pull down on the overhead cord.
- c. I push down on the foot pedal.
- d. Hey, you're making this up. The ride just goes in a circle, not up and down.

5. This ride sometimes has to shut down due to the forces of nature. Look at the Zephyr. What do you think would cause Disney to close it for the day?

    a. Rain
    b. Strong wind
    c. Cold
    d. Heat

6. Collection Time! If you still have time before your Zephyr ride, this would be a great time to work on a Collection. T-shirts and backpacks would work well here.

Goofy's Sky School

1. Did you notice the sign for this ride as you walked up? Something hangs beneath it. What is it?

    a. Goofy himself   b. A chicken
    c. A plane   d. A propeller

2. The sign advises you of the "way to fly." What does it say?

    a. Fly Like A Chicken
    b. Fly The Goofy Way!
    c. Flap Your Arms!
    d. Up, of course.

3. Someone is giving you a thumbs up through a window. Who?

    a. Goofy
    b. A friendly chicken—wait, do chickens have thumbs?
    c. Mickey Mouse
    d. What window?

4. Oh my, it looks like there has been a delivery of eggs. Where are they from?
   a. Fresh from Goofy's Farm; that guy gets around.
   b. From Chickenlands Best
   c. From a chicken, I expect. Or maybe the egg came first? It's hard to say.
   d. Who cares? I want an omelet.
   e. Both 'a' and 'c'

5. How are they delivered?
   a. By Goofy's Trucking and Freight
   b. By chicken, I see them nesting on top of the crates.
   c. By airmail, naturally
   d. Who cares? Now about that omelet…

6. There is something unusual about those chickens. What is it?
   a. They look like normal chickens to me.
   b. They are roosters and yet they seem to be laying eggs. Hmm.
   c. They are purple, and I'm sorry, but that's not a normal color for a chicken.
   d. Well, they are wearing goggles and flying hats. That's not something you see every day.

7. Something appears to be upside down. What?
   a. An airplane flown by Goofy
   b. An egg carton, all the eggs are falling out! So much for my omelet.
   c. Goofy's flying license
   d. All of the above
   e. Both 'a' and 'b'

8. Treasure Hunt Time! See how many of these Goofy treasures you can find before it is time to take to the skies.

- ❑ A blue patch
- ❑ A bolt of lightning
- ❑ The number 2
- ❑ Three hens a-laying
- ❑ A purple shell
- ❑ Mickey Mouse
- ❑ Instructions that Captain Hook would not like
- ❑ A place for ground crew only
- ❑ A bar code
- ❑ A fishy exit sign
- ❑ A white scarf
- ❑ A tower of sunshine
- ❑ A yellow arrow
- ❑ Two brains
- ❑ A jellyfish
- ❑ A propeller not attached to a plane
- ❑ A hook
- ❑ Two ways to tell wind direction
- ❑ An egg
- ❑ A tack
- ❑ A white tassel

9. Have a look at the picture of Goofy flying upside down. What's wrong with his plane?

a. The propeller has stopped turning.

b. The wing has a crack in it.

c. There is a patch on one of the landing wheels.

d. All of the above are true, but I am sure Goofy can handle it.

10. Two of the chickens in this picture are missing something that the others have. What did they forget? **FP**

a. Their hats

b. How to fly

c. Their goggles

d. Their feathers; they're naked!

11. Look around for Goofy's official business permit. What is his permit for exactly? **FP**
    a. A flight school, naturally
    b. Oh no, a chicken farm!
    c. Whatever he wants
    d. Patting his head and rubbing his tummy

12. What must you have if you want to learn to fly like a bird? **FP**
    a. Courage; you can't be a chicken.
    b. Wings would be helpful.
    c. The desire to learn and the school registration fee of some chicken feed and an ear of corn, extra butter
    d. A bird brain

13. When maneuvering your plane down, which of these things should you do? **FP**
    a. Push the stick forward.
    b. Close your eyes.
    c. Scream.
    d. All of the above
    e. Only 'b' and 'c'

14. What does effective braking prevent? **FP**
    a. Defective braking
    b. Crashing
    c. Boo-boos
    d. Failure to stop

15. According to Babbitt Employment Agency, what will you be qualified to do after graduating from Goofy's Sky School? **FP**
    a. Egg farming
    b. Fly a plane
    c. Rodeo clowning
    d. Absolutely nothing
    e. All of the above

16. What costs $48? **FP**
   a. A crate of eggs suitable for throwing
   b. Lowest grade flight fuel
   c. One flight lesson at Goofy's Sky School
   d. Optional landing gear rental

17. Goofy is selling a parachute. How is it described? **FP**
   a. Only used once, never opened
   b. Constructed entirely of old pants
   c. Easily fixed (It only has one big rip.)
   d. As is, best when used on the ground

18. What is number 80254? **FP**
   a. Goofy's pilot license number
   b. The patent number for The Flying Contraption
   c. The chicken and egg population at Goofy's Farm, oh I mean Flight School
   d. Goofy's lucky number; what's yours?

19. According to the weather gram, what weather can you expect in the next several days? **FP**
   a. Sunny with temperatures hot enough to fry an egg
   b. Hurricane force feather storms; it is inadvisable for student pilots to be in the air.
   c. Cloudy with 100% chance of falling eggs from the north
   d. Breezy with a 90% chance of chickens

20. What may impede your flying lesson? **FP**
   a. Flying chickens (but only if you egg them on)
   b. The instructor (You have been warned.)
   c. Your flying contraption is not guaranteed to stay airborne.
   d. All of the above
   e. Only 'b' and 'c'

21. How many of the required courses has Goofy completed to become a flight instructor? **FP**

    a. Enough
    b. All
    c. Most
    d. None

22. Treasure Hunt Time! You are very close to take-off. See if you can find these treasures before they fly away. **FP**

- ❑ A chicken holding a bucket
- ❑ A barrel of nails
- ❑ A hammer
- ❑ A frightened cow
- ❑ A chicken holding a flag
- ❑ Two springs
- ❑ A flag with Goofy on it
- ❑ A big spill
- ❑ A flock of ducks
- ❑ A bi-plane (a plane with two sets of wings)
- ❑ A chicken with a parachute
- ❑ A scarecrow
- ❑ A student pilot
- ❑ An egg carton with a new purpose
- ❑ Goofy delivering eggs by airmail
- ❑ Footy pajamas
- ❑ A broken propeller
- ❑ A chicken-feed bag that has a new job

Jumpin' Jellyfish

1. There are a lot of jellyfish in this kelp forest. Can you find one that is yellow with yellow spots?

   Yes / No

2. These jellyfish come in lots of bright colors. Which of the jellyfish described below is not in this kelp forest?
   - a. Yellow with orange stripes and pink openings
   - b. Pink with blue stripes and yellow openings
   - c. Pink with orange stripes and green openings
   - d. Orange with pink stripes and blue openings

3. Are there any jellyfish here that aren't jumping?

   Yes / No

4. What creature is being used to measure the height of jellyfish jumpers?
   - a. A starfish
   - b. A jellyfish
   - c. A school of fish
   - d. A seahorse

5. Treasure Hunt Time! Find these kelp forest treasures before you spring into action.
   - ❏ Kelp berries
   - ❏ Three yellow seahorses
   - ❏ Blue tentacles
   - ❏ A school of orange fish
   - ❏ At least five pink starfish
   - ❏ Escaping air
   - ❏ The imprint of a starfish

- ❏ The imprint of a shell
- ❏ Something shiny and silver
- ❏ A gold roof
- ❏ A bright green fence

King Triton's Carousel

1. King Triton has a beautiful instrument near his carousel. What is it?
   a. A piano
   b. A calliope (an instrument with steam whistles that look like pipes)
   c. A harp (an instrument with many strings, often large)
   d. A water flute

2. What animals can be found going round and round on King Triton's Carousel? Check off all that are correct.

a. Sea Otter	b. Manatee
c. Seahorse	d. Seal
e. Shark	f. Dolphin
g. Octopus	h. Whale
i. Sea snail	j. Two kinds of fish
k. Crab	

3. One of the animals brought a snack for later. Which animal is it?

a. Seahorse	b. Whale
c. Dolphin	d. Sea Otter

4. One animal is very proud of his workplace. He is holding up a banner for Paradise Pier. Which animal is it?

a. Seal	b. Octopus
c. Fish	d. Crab

5. One of the animals is sporting a lovely seaweed ensemble. Which one?
  a. Dolphin
  b. Seal
  c. Sea Otter
  d. Whale

6. When was Santa Monica Pier established?
  a. 1904
  b. 1923
  c. 1952
  d. 1968

7. One of the saddled animals is depicted without any flippers at all. Which one?
  a. Whale
  b. Sea Otter
  c. Seal
  d. Seahorse

8. Treasure Hunt Time! See if you can spot these deep sea treasures before you swim away.
  ❑ Barnacles
  ❑ A small gold trident
  ❑ Gold flowers
  ❑ A dolphin with fancy gold-and-green painted designs adorning him
  ❑ A blue jewel
  ❑ A yellow jewel
  ❑ A red jewel
  ❑ A pink jewel
  ❑ A clear jewel
  ❑ A green jewel
  ❑ A pearl
  ❑ A gold mermaid
  ❑ A large pink shell

Mickey's Fun Wheel

1. What are your options when choosing a gondola to ride on the Fun Wheel? Circle all that apply.
   - a. Swinging gondola
   - b. Flipping gondola
   - c. Non-swinging gondola
   - d. Spinning gondola

2. There are some very fancy benches facing the water near this ride. What is special about them?
   - a. They can spin to face any direction you wish.
   - b. They are shaped like the ride gondolas, but they are on the pier.
   - c. They are made of canvas, tilted back, and have footrests.
   - d. They are made of sea creatures.

3. Treasure Hunt Time! There's a lot to look at here in all directions. This list will begin with things you can find looking toward the pier itself and end with things to find looking out over the water. The pier view disappears faster so it's a good idea to collect those things first.
   - ❏ Someone breathing fire
   - ❏ An eagle
   - ❏ A polka-dot shirt
   - ❏ A bearded lady
   - ❏ The letter P in a circle
   - ❏ A lady wearing a snake as an accessory
   - ❏ A lock
   - ❏ Two peacocks
   - ❏ A giant pointing finger
   - ❏ A handlebar mustache

- ❑ A man eating something he definitely shouldn't
- ❑ A big red bow
- ❑ Musical notes in gold
- ❑ Green kelp
- ❑ A giant billboard featuring a girl and her dog
- ❑ A trident
- ❑ An enormous set of teeth
- ❑ A straw hat with a red flower sticking out of it

4. Someone appears to be conducting a symphony. What is he wearing?
   a. A black tux, gray shoes, and top hat
   b. A long red coat, yellow shoes, and red hat with a feather
   c. A purple tail coat with jeweled buttons, green shoes, and purple wizard's hat
   d. Red-and-white striped footy pajamas with the backflap half open and matching sleeping cap

5. Just prior to climbing into your gondola, there is a warning. What is it?
   a. "Lower your head."
   b. "Don't rock the gondola."
   c. "Don't climb on the gondola."
   d. All of the above

6. The gondolas all feature pictures of famous Disney characters. Cross off all of the characters you can find on the gondolas.
   a. Mickey Mouse   b. Goofy
   c. Chip 'n Dale   d. Donald Duck
   e. Ludwig Von Drake   f. Daisy Duck
   g. Pluto   h. Minnie Mouse
   i. Clarabelle Cow

7. What other rides can you see from this line? Earn 1 point for each ride you spot. _____

Silly Symphony Swings

1. What is unique about the letter "S" as it appears on the Silly Symphony Swings sign?
   a. It is not capitalized.
   b. It is formed of wind and is blowing away.
   c. It is a musical clef sign.
   d. It looks like a normal "S" to me.

2. The Silly Symphony players appear to be in a bit of trouble. What is happening to them?
   a. There appears to be a volcano erupting.
   b. They are in a tornado.
   c. They are in a tidal wave.
   d. They have forgotten how to play the "William Tell Overture."

3. For safety reasons, people can't take their bags on the swings with them. Where do they store their things while they go for a spin?
   a. In the seat pouches under the swings
   b. In the cubby shelves provided
   c. In the baskets on the ground
   d. They must leave all carry-on items with a friend.

4. Can a child ride with a parent?
   a. Yes, there are some double seats.
   b. No, all riders must face the storm independently.

5. Who plays the tuba?
   a. Donald Duck
   b. A pig
   c. A cow
   d. Mickey Mouse

6. Several birds have been disrupted by this symphonic storm. Which of the following best describes the birds' perilous situation?
   a. Four birds are holding on to a broken branch.
   b. One bird is in a teacup and two others are in a saucer.
   c. Two birds are in a nest and another is flying away.
   d. Three birds are holding onto Mickey's head for dear life. Don't they know they can fly?

7. Treasure Hunt Time! See how many of these wind-swept treasures you can locate before you blow away yourself.
   - ❑   Three horseshoes
   - ❑   A blue chair
   - ❑   An upside-down flute player
   - ❑   A bench
   - ❑   A broom
   - ❑   Someone riding a tuba
   - ❑   A Mickey Mouse glove
   - ❑   Sheet music
   - ❑   An arrow
   - ❑   A dedicated drummer
   - ❑   Donald Duck
   - ❑   A white hat
   - ❑   A cow with a big mouth
   - ❑   Mickey Mouse
   - ❑   A basket of fruit
   - ❑   A panicked chicken

The Little Mermaid

Outside Queue

1. It is time to play **Scuttle Says**.

   When Ariel finds new human treasures she takes them to her seagull friend Scuttle for identification. Scuttle fancies himself knowledgeable about all things human. When presented with a human item he makes up a crazy name for it. Then he tells what it is used for. He is always wrong.

   Today Ariel can't find Scuttle, so it is up to you to help her out. Here is a list of human treasures you may find on the guests in line with you. When you find one you must give it a name. For example, when presented with a fork, Scuttle called it a "dingulhopper". He went on to tell how humans use dingulhoppers to straighten their hair.

   To earn your points you must find a human treasure, name it, and tell what it is used for. You get 1 point for each treasure that you find, rename, and give a silly purpose to.

   Find:
   - ☐ Cell phone
   - ☐ Drink cup
   - ☐ Book
   - ☐ Glasses
   - ☐ Headband
   - ☐ Hat
   - ☐ Purse
   - ☐ Balloon
   - ☐ Backpack

- ❑ Watch
- ❑ Bandana
- ❑ Toy
- ❑ Necklace
- ❑ Lanyard
- ❑ Brush or comb
- ❑ Camera
- ❑ Coat
- ❑ Pen
- ❑ Snack

Inside Queue

2. Treasure Hunt Time! It is almost time for you to swim away, but before you do, see if you can find these last few of Ariel's missing treasures.

- ❑ A telescope
- ❑ Three tridents
- ❑ A crow's nest
- ❑ Two starfish in different places
- ❑ Someone with their tongue out
- ❑ A blue glass ball
- ❑ A windmill
- ❑ A seagull
- ❑ Two lanterns
- ❑ Coral
- ❑ A rope
- ❑ A crab
- ❑ A green shell with blue lining

Toy Story Midway Mania!

1. As you enter the queue, which of these items does not appear to be for sale on the Boardwalk?
   - a. Jelly beans
   - b. Churros
   - c. Turkey legs
   - d. Newspapers

2. Look ahead to where you board the ride. There are pictures of toys. Which of these toys are in the picture?
   - a. A toy dinosaur
   - b. A toy horse
   - c. A toy cannon
   - d. All of them
   - e. All but 'c'

? Mr. Potato Head Pop Quiz!

You should soon see Mr. Potato Head. He will perform to keep you entertained while you wait. Enjoy his show (it is hilarious). When you are no longer close enough to hear his routine, play this memory game. (Don't feel bad if you can't get them all. His routine is very long, so you will only hear some of it.) If you don't know the answer, take a guess. Or circle it and try answering it later if you ride Toy Story Mania again.

Do you remember what you heard?

3. When Mr. Potato Head says "Well at least you are honest," what is he referring to?
   - a. The fact that you like French fries
   - b. The fact that you don't want to raise your hand anymore
   - c. The fact that you do not think he is particularly skinny
   - d. The fact that you don't think Mr. Potato Head was the star of *Toy Story*

4. What is it time to do while Andy is away?
  a. "It's time to find moving buddies; I claim Mrs. Potato Head!"
  b. "It's time for a meeting of the toys."
  c. "It's time to play."
  d. "It's time to prepare for Andy's birthday party. Has anyone seen the Army Men?"

5. For Mr. Potato Head, what is Midway Mania more fun than?
  a. A day with all of his pieces in the right spot
  b. The first day Andy played with him
  c. A day without drool; when is that baby going to stop teething anyway?
  d. A barrel of monkeys

6. What does Mr. Potato Head do to make people happy?
  a. He pulls off his ear.
  b. He sings a song.
  c. He stops singing a song.
  d. He offers to introduce everybody to Buzz and Woody next time they are around.

7. What makes him a commentator?
  a. He has a microphone and you are listening.
  b. He is a potato and he makes comments.
  c. Have you ever encountered an uncommentator?
  d. To be a commentator you have to have a pretty big head, and he is all head.

8. Mr. Potato Head tells you that there is nothing to be afraid of and that you should trust him. Why?
  a. If he is lying, you can take his mouth off.
  b. Potatoes never tell a lie.
  c. If there was something to fear he would have spotted it: he has lots of eyes.
  d. He is a hot potato.

9. What does Mr. Potato Head think that you might have in your ears?

    a. Potatoes

    b. Wax

    c. A Green Army Man

    d. Toothpaste

10. What is Mr. Potato Head hoping that someone will say about him?

    a. That spuds make the best friends

    b. That he is trustworthy

    c. That he is their favorite toy

    d. That he should be elected head toy; after all he's all head

11. Mr. Potato Head makes a comment about Buzz that is between you and him. What is it?

    a. Buzz needs new batteries.

    b. Buzz can be a little bit spacey.

    c. Buzz is out to lunch.

    d. Buzz is a little bit nervous about traveling to infinity and beyond.

12. What or who whined a little when stepped on by Rex the dinosaur?

    a. A grape

    b. Woody

    c. The squeaky ball

    d. Himself: he stepped on his own foot.

13. Why can't Mr. Potato Head hear you?

    a. He is all eyes, not all ears.

    b. He pulled his ear out.

    c. How well would you hear with a plastic ear?

    d. Because he never stops talking

14. How does Mr. Potato Head tell you that the games will be in 3-D?

    a. He raises and lowers a flashcard with a D on it three times.

b. He puts on 3-D glasses.

c. He sings a little song about the 3-D games on the midway.

d. He asks you to give him a "D" three times and then asks, "What have you got?"

15. Mr. Potato Head offers to guess someone's weight. What is his guess?

a. 100 potatoes

b. More than a barrel of monkeys but less than the refrigerator

c. 20 to 30 minutes

d. Mr. Potato Head never guesses weight. That would be rude.

16. Mr. Potato Head offers you a hint. What is it?

a. "This is the part where you clap."

b. "Be sure to pull the trigger."

c. "Keep your eye on the ball."

d. "Be sure to put your glasses on."

17. What can you call Mr. Potato Head?

a. Spuds   b. Mr. Potato Head

c. Mr. Idaho   d. The world's best toy

18. What does Mr. Potato Head ask you to shout?

a. I will never become a vegetarian.

b. I love vegetables!

c. I love you Mr. Potato Head!

d. Mr. Potato Head is my favorite toy!

19. What did Mr. Potato Head's new hat cost him?

a. It was free with proof of purchase.

b. An arm and a leg

c. $3.99 plus tax

d. Respect, he lost it when he put that silly thing on.

20. What does he love most about being Mr. Potato Head?
- a. Mrs. Potato Head
- b. Getting dressed is a snap.
- c. He's got lots of parts.
- d. Changing the way he looks is child's play.

21. Why shouldn't Mrs. Potato Head get plastic surgery?
- a. What if the surgeon is in the mood for French fries?
- b. Potatoes are supposed to be round.
- c. Potatoes shouldn't have surgery, they are too thin skinned.
- d. She has three noses already.

Do you remember what you saw?

22. What kind of hat was Mr. Potato Head wearing?
- a. A straw hat
- b. A bowler (an old-fashioned hat with a round top and brim)
- c. A baseball cap
- d. A bonnet

23. Was Mr. Potato Head wearing gloves?
- a. Yes, black
- b. Yes, white
- c. Yes, red
- d. No, he had bare hands.

24. Was Mr. Potato Head wearing shoes?
- a. Yes, black and shiny
- b. Yes, tiny
- c. Yes, men's gray dress shoes
- d. Do potatoes have feet?

25. Did Mr. Potato Head have a mustache?
Yes / No

26. There were buttons somewhere on Mr. Potato Head's clothes. Where were they?
    a. On his cuffs
    b. Around the rim of his hat
    c. On his spats (the white covers on his shoes)
    d. On his shirt front. Wait a minute, that potato had no shirt!

27. There was a power button to push on his display, what did it say?
    a. "Push here."
    b. "Try Me!"
    c. "Start."
    d. "Sometimes you really push my buttons!" (Get it? "my buttons")

28. What was in Mr. Potato Head's hand?
    a. A microphone
    b. An extra part
    c. A cane
    d. Nothing

29. Did Mr. Potato Head ever change body parts?
    Yes / No

30. Did Mr. Potato Head have a trapdoor opening on his back side for parts storage?
    Yes / No

31. What color were Mr. Potato Head's sleeves?
    a. Green-and-white striped
    b. White
    c. Red-and-white striped
    d. I already told you, that potato wasn't wearing a shirt.

32. What was Mr. Potato Head's title as it was printed on his stage?
   a. "World's Only Talking Potato"
   b. "World's Best Toy"
   c. "Andy's Favorite"
   d. "Boardwalk Barker"

This is the end of Mr. Potato Pop Quiz.

Poster Area

33. Check out the poster for Woody's Rootin' Tootin' Shootin' Gallery. How many darts are on it?
   a. 1   b. 2
   c. 3   d. 4

34. How many bull's-eyes are on the poster?
   a. 4   b. 5
   c. 6   d. 7

35. What must you do to win at Dino Darts?
   a. Pop a balloon.
   b. Throw a ring around the dinosaur's neck.
   c. Hit a dino on the head.
   d. All of the above

36. What is the orange liquid in the picture?
   a. Slime
   b. Lava
   c. Spilled punch
   d. None of the above

37. There were targets on this poster with point values marked on them. How many points do you get per target?
   a. 100 each
   b. 500 each
   c. 1,000 each
   d. All of the above

38. What should you do to your shooter in the ride to make it launch farther?
    a. Pull back farther on the string.
    b. Aim lower.
    c. Aim higher.
    d. You cannot change how far it launches.

39. On the how-to-play poster, what is coming out of the shooter?
    a. Rings   b. A ball
    c. Both   d. Neither

40. Plates with stars on them are the targets on whose poster?
    a. The Pink Pig's
    b. Woody and Jessie's
    c. Buzz Lightyear's
    d. The Green Army Men's

41. What are the Green Army Men hanging on?
    a. Jump rope   b. Parachutes
    c. Each other   d. The end of a train
                          of linking monkeys

42. What is being tossed at the sitting ducks in the game Hamm and Eggs?
    a. Rings   b. Darts
    c. Colored eggs   d. Bread crumbs

43. Which poster features a unicorn?
    a. Green Army Men Shooting Camp
    b. Hamm and Eggs
    c. Woody's Rootin' Tootin' Shootin' Gallery
    d. Rex & Trixie's Dino Darts

44. What does Buzz want you to do?
    a. "Ring an Alien in Outer Space."
    b. "Shoot Straight, Space Rangers."
    c. "Come With Me to Infinity and Beyond."
    d. "Make Me Proud."

45. Who was waving at you from Buzz's poster?
   a. An alien
   b. Buzz
   c. A unicorn
   d. No one waved. That was a space salute.

46. There is something out of place in the area where you pick up your 3-D glasses. What is it?
   a. A peep hole
   b. There are curtains but no window.
   c. Sea life
   d. All of the above

47. Treasure Hunt Time! See how many of these playthings you can put away before you start your game.
   - ❑ Rex the dinosaur
   - ❑ A game card with a seahorse on it
   - ❑ The letter F
   - ❑ The words "Play Set"
   - ❑ A toy microphone
   - ❑ Bo Peep
   - ❑ Mr. Potato Head
   - ❑ Jessie
   - ❑ Hamm
   - ❑ Bullseye
   - ❑ Space alien

Paradise Pier Answers

California Screamin' Billboards

Billboard 1: Coca-Cola

1) d. Delicious and Refreshing
2) Yes
3) b. Her mom
4) a. Several bottles of Coke
5) No
6) b. Yes, a lady
7) c. A white dress, hat, socks, and buckle shoes
8) False
9) b. A bottle of Coke
10) Yes
11) No
12) a. Yes
13) c. It was in a short blond bob.
14) d. 8

Billboard 2: Garden Dining

1) f. Only 'a' and 'c'
2) No
3) b. Looked like a mug of beer
4) a. A blue blouse, a blue skirt thigh length, and a half apron. Oh, and a hat
5) Yes
6) No
7) c. A cameo
8) a. No there was a boy, too.
9) No
10) Yes
11) No
12) d. Live Music
13) b. By the Bay

Billboard 3: Soar

1) c. Soar at the shore.
2) b. Golden Zephyr and Silly Symphony Swings
3) No

California Screamin': *Billboard 3: Soar, cont'd.*

4) Yes
5) d. A bird
6) Yes
7) a. Conducting
8) d. What wings?
9) c. Conducting
10) True
11) False
12) c. Flying

Billboard 4: Paradise Pier

1) d. Standing on a balcony looking out at the ocean
2) b. An old-fashioned purple dress
3) b. A green striped suit with a tie
4) Yes
5) d. No, there were no pets.
6) Yes
7) c. Sea gulls
8) a. Umbrellas
9) No
10) Yes
11) c. Yes, in and under a three-story shelter
12) d. Between Sea and Sky
13) a. Of course. It was the roller coaster, right?

Golden Zephyr

1-2) The answers depend on your family.
3) Total Treasures found _____
4) d. Hey, you're making this up. The ride just goes in a circle, not up and down.
5) b. Strong wind
6) Number of items collected _____

Goofy's Sky School

1) d. A propeller
2) b. Fly The Goofy Way!
3) b. A friendly chicken
4) a. Fresh from Goofy's Farm
5) c. By airmail
6) d. They are wearing goggles and a flying hat.
7) a. An airplane flown by Goofy
8) Total Goofy Treasures found _____

9) c. There is a patch on one of the landing wheels.
10) a. Their hats
11) b. A chicken farm
12) d. A bird brain
13) d. All of the above
14) a. Defective braking
15) c. Rodeo clowning
16) b. Lowest grade flight fuel
17) a. Only used once, never opened
18) b. The patent number
19) d. Breezy with a 90% chance of chickens
20) a. Flying chickens
21) a. Enough
22) Total Preflight Treasures found _____

Jumpin' Jellyfish
1) Yes
2) c. Pink with orange stripes and green openings
3) Yes
4) a. A starfish
5) Total Treasures found _____

King Triton's Carousel
1) b. A calliope
2) a. Sea Otter, c. Seahorse, d. Seal, f. Dolphin,
   g. Octopus, h. Whale, j. Two kinds of fish
3) d. Sea Otter
4) b. Octopus
5) c. Sea Otter
6) b. 1923
7) d. Seahorse
8) Total Treasures found _____

Mickey's Fun Wheel
1) a. Swinging gondola and c. Non-swinging gondola
2) d. They are made of sea creatures.
3) Total Treasures found _____
4) b. A long red coat, yellow shoes, and red hat with a feather
5) a. "Lower your head."
6) a. Mickey, b. Goofy, d. Donald, g. Pluto, h. Minnie
7) Number of other rides spotted _____

Silly Symphony Swings

1) c. It is a musical clef sign.
2) b. They are in a tornado.
3) c. In the baskets on the ground
4) a. Yes
5) b. A pig
6) c. Two birds are in a nest and another is flying away.
7) Total Treasures found _____

The Little Mermaid

1) Scuttle Says points:
   Player 1 _____, Player 2 _____,
   Player 3 _____, Player 4 _____
Inside Queue
2) Total Treasures found _____

Toy Story Midway Mania!

1) a. Jelly beans
2) d. All of them
Mr. Potato Head Pop Quiz (Answers 3 to 32)
3) b. The fact that you don't want to raise your hand anymore
4) c. "It's time to play."
5) d. A barrel of monkeys
6) a. He pulls off his ear.
7) b. He is a potato and he makes comments.
8) d. He is a hot potato.
9) a. Potatoes
10) c. That he is their favorite toy
11) c. Buzz is out to lunch.
12) a. A grape
13) b. He pulled his ear out.
14) d. He asks you to give him a "D" three times and then asks, "What have you got?"
15) c. 20 to 30 minutes
16) a. "This is the part where you clap."
17) b. Mr. Potato Head
18) c. I love you Mr. Potato Head!
19) b. An arm and a leg
20) b. Getting dressed is a snap.
21) d. She has three noses already.

22) a. A straw hat
23) b. Yes, white
24) a. Yes, black and shiny
25) Yes
26) a. On his cuffs
27) b. "Try Me!"
28) a. A microphone
29) No
30) Yes
31) c. Red-and-white striped
32) d. "Boardwalk Barker"

Poster Area

33) b. 2
34) c. 6
35) a. Pop a balloon.
36) b. Lava
37) a. 100 each
38) c. Aim higher.
39) c. Both
40) d. The Green Army Men's
41) a. Jump Rope
42) c. Colored eggs
43) b. Hamm and Eggs
44) a. "Ring an Alien in Outer Space."
45) b. Buzz
46) d. All of the above
47) Total Treasures found _____

Disney California Adventure Scavenger Hunt

You can hunt for the treasures below as you walk from attraction to attraction. Or if you prefer, you can devote part of your day to finding these treasures. Either way, keep your eyes open to rack up more points. Happy Hunting!

Paradise Pier

- ☐ A giant sand dollar
- ☐ A see-through Donald Duck playing the flute
- ☐ A rabbit in a hat
- ☐ A yellow mailbox
- ☐ A rather flat baseball
- ☐ An elephant with a feather in his trunk
- ☐ A toy package big enough for you
- ☐ A magazine called *Modern Priscilla*
- ☐ A black carousel horse
- ☐ A bumper car, not shaped like a ladybug
- ☐ Address 64

Pacific Wharf

- ☐ A giant vat of olive oil
- ☐ 7¼ tons of fish
- ☐ A dragon
- ☐ Pottery hanging upside-down

"a bug's land"

- ❑ A school of blue fish and gold fish
- ❑ An ant checking you out with a telescope
- ❑ A stick bug hiding
- ❑ A giant paperclip
- ❑ A watermelon arch
- ❑ A restroom sign made from corrugated cardboard
- ❑ A bench made from Popsicle sticks

Hollywood Land

- ❑ The way to valet parking
- ❑ Five hotdogs with top hats
- ❑ A sky that is always cloudy
- ❑ A fire hydrant with bling
- ❑ Ben Hair
- ❑ A mosaic containing a piano, a spoon, and an avocado pit
- ❑ A gold comb and hairbrush

Condor Flats

- ❑ An airplane making a big mess

Grizzly Peak

- ❑ A deer-crossing sign
- ❑ 5 cents for a cold shower
- ❑ A water wheel
- ❑ A bear getting a piggyback ride
- ❑ A bear wearing a backpack
- ❑ Mining car No. 9
- ❑ California's state flag
- ❑ The snowmobile route
- ❑ Eureka mine shaft No. 2

Cars Land

- ❑ A gold tooth
- ❑ Traffic court
- ❑ A place to get Party Ice
- ❑ An Easy Idle Multi pack
- ❑ Two brick cars
- ❑ Four dice

Cars Land, cont'd.

- ☐ A cocktail for those who feel like a nut
- ☐ R.S. Municipal Code 20.12
- ☐ A pill with a 'G' on it
- ☐ A truck on a spring
- ☐ A big U.S. flag
- ☐ A cone of light
- ☐ A stegosaurus
- ☐ A yellow traffic light
- ☐ A sale of $3.33
- ☐ A paint sprayer
- ☐ A TV antenna
- ☐ Corn-fed soy
- ☐ An 8-ball

Buena Vista Street

- ☐ Destination Hollywood
- ☐ A crate of baseballs
- ☐ "Surley" Verne Hoffman
- ☐ A diving helmet
- ☐ Three flutes
- ☐ A caged bird
- ☐ A paintbrush with green paint on the tip
- ☐ A sweet mountain
- ☐ A finger purse
- ☐ A mouse with a bag
- ☐ A tile man
- ☐ A ticket booth

Disney California Adventure Scavenger Hunt Tally

Total Treasures found _____

Acknowledgements

I want to offer my sincere thanks to all of my friends and family who made it possible for me to achieve this goal. Thanks first and foremost to my husband Ken Pierce, my guru of all things technical! Thank you to my daughter Camille Pierce, for providing what no one else did, a kid's perspective. Thank you to my mother Carol Curtis for trips to the park, hours of work, and a level of support that is a gift. Without your unwavering support this book would never have happened.

Many people offered their help along the way to this book becoming a reality. I hope I will remember you all here, but if you are not named specifically, please know that your help was nonetheless deeply appreciated.

Thank you to Michele Dodds, for the gift of your art for my web page. You are so very talented and have such a giving heart.

Thanks as well to Katy, Dan, Gillian, Annie, and Sam Duncan for trying out my work for the first time at Disneyland. Your words of enjoyment were a gift.

Thank you to Kevin Hall, Johann Salloom, Lindsey Hall, and especially Alana Hall for making Camille so happy and comfortable while I traveled. It is impossible to emphasize enough what a help that was.

Thank you to Gia Gordon for giving Camille something fun to do after school.

Thank you to my many friend and family

readers for your honest input on my idea and my work. You helped me get this book in motion, Dick Curtis, Dick Debberthine, Caterina D'Agrosa, Skip Volkmann, Cristen Miller, Hillary Egna, Erin DeBoard, Eric DeBoard.

Thank you to my grandfather Nero Roy whose Christmas gift helped take me on the next part of this journey.

Thank you to Jay Burzinski whose birthday and Christmas gifts did likewise and of course the frequent flyer miles.

Thank you to best friend Lisa Book for your level of constant enthusiasm and excitement about my project. You helped keep me pumped more then you will ever know or believe.

Thank you to all of the friends I bored constantly with never-ending updates on how the book was going. You are the best.

And a big thank you to Jennifer Arnold, Heather Lowe, and Vashti Martin-Hatfield for your awesome photography skills. You speeded my research and helped me stay on top of changes.

Thanks to The Intrepid Traveler for seeing the magic I see in the lines at Disney. Thank you to my editor Sally Scanlon for tirelessly listening to my concerns and to cover designer George Foster and interior designer Tim Foster for making my book beautiful.

Finally thank you to the Disney Corporation for making such awesome places to play. I love Disneyland and Walt Disney World. I think that they are a gift to everyone lucky enough to visit them.

Index

The following abbreviations appear in this Index:

DL – Disneyland Park
CA – Disney California Adventure Park

You'll find each ride listed alphabetically, as well as by "land" or "area" for easy lookup.

A

B

C

D

E

F

G

H

About The Author

Meredith L. Pierce was born in England but grew up in Disneyland's vast backyard, Orange County, California. She was introduced to Disney magic at a very young age and enjoyed regular visits to the park as a child, teenager, and adult. Like millions of people, Meredith loved Disneyland from the moment she laid eyes on it. The creativity, attention to detail, and positive environment kept her returning year after year.

In due time, Meredith graduated from The College of Communications at California State University Fullerton and spent the next 15 years working to improve the lives of children and

Photo by Carol Curtis

adults with developmental disabilities and mental illness. Her jobs varied from helping people find and keep meaningful employment to finding ways for them to live independently with appropriate assistance. She was also responsible for creating a large portion of the staff training curriculum used by North Carolina's biggest provider of services for individuals with these challenges.

The inspiration for *Lots To Do In Line Disneyland* came to Meredith during her first trip to Disneyland with her own daughter, then age seven. Looking at the park in the role of Mommy made her notice things she had failed to register before. The lines were a wonderland of things to see and do, and they were going unnoticed and underappreciated. One year later, *Lots To Do In Line Disneyland* was born.

The Disneyland parks are constantly changing—adding new attractions and renovating and replacing others. If you spot a new visual in the queue lines or notice that one has disappeared, I hope you will let me know through my website:

www.LotsTo Do InLine.com

Thanks for your help. Sharing your knowledge will make these games even more fun for everyone.

— Meredith Pierce

P.S. If you're headed for Walt Disney World sometime in the future, be sure to get a copy of *Lots To Do In Line Walt Disney World*. It'll make your waits there as much fun as I hope this book made them in Disneyland.

You can download a free excerpt from:

http://intrepidtraveler.com/download-free-excerpts/